GLOBAL SNAPS

500 PHOTOGRAPHS FROM 7 CONTINENTS

Udaipur, India

GLOBAL SNAPS

500 PHOTOGRAPHS FROM 7 CONTINENTS

MICHAEL CLINTON

FOREWORD BY PAMELA FIORI

Glitterati
INCORPORATED
NEW YORK, NEW YORK

First published in the United States of America
in 2005 by Glitterati Incorporated

Glitterati
INCORPORATED

225 Central Park West, New York, New York 10024
Telephone 212-362-9119/Fax 212-362-7174
www.GlitteratiIncorporated.com

Distributed in North America by powerHouse Books,
a division of powerHouse Cultural Entertainment, Inc.
68 Charlton Street, New York, NY 10014-4601
Telephone 212-604-9074, fax 212-366-5247
email: GlobalSnaps@powerHouseBooks.com;
web site: www.powerHouseBooks.com

First edition, 2005
Library of Congress Control Number: **2005926197**
Hardcover ISBN **0-9765851-1-1**

Design: Karen Engelmann, Luminary Books & Design

Printed and bound in China by
Hong Kong Graphics & Printing Ltd.

10 9 8 7 6 5 4 3 2 1

This book is dedicated
to the next generation
of travelers...
Shannon, Clint, Sean,
Luke, Paul, Molly,
David, Bobby,
and Nicolas.
Enjoy the journey!

Architectural detail, Malmö, Sweden

CONTENTS

FOREWORD
Pamela Fiori

9

INTRODUCTION
Michael Clinton

10

Eiffel Tower, Paris, France

ANTARCTICA   13
Antarctic Peninsula

SOUTH AMERICA   53
Argentina, Bolivia,
Colombia, Ecuador, Peru

NORTH AMERICA   87
Anguilla, Costa Rica, Cuba,
Mexico, United States

EUROPE   139
Croatia, Denmark, France, Greece,
Ireland, Italy, Turkey, United Kingdom

AFRICA   203
Egypt, Morocco, Namibia
South Africa, Tanzania, Tunisia

OCEANIA   251
Australia, Fiji

ASIA   283
Bhutan, Cambodia, China,
Hong Kong, India, Indonesia,
Japan, Myanmar (Burma), Nepal,
Thailand, Vietnam

Windmills, Mykonos, Greece

8

FOREWORD

Pamela Fiori

The photographs you are about to see are the result of more than a quarter of a century of picture taking on the run. Michael Clinton is, by nature and by discipline, someone who works quickly and strategically, with no wasted movements. This is true with just about everything he does in his fast-paced and varied life. An executive vice-president of Hearst Magazines and overseeing no fewer than sixteen titles and their publishers, Clinton can hone in on a problem and solve it within seconds—without a moment's hesitation or indecision. He is a practicing aviator whose reflexes are quick and accurate. He is an undaunted adventurer for whom no place is too far and no situation too risky. When he travels, whether for business or for his own pleasure, he's a man with a plan, making the most of whatever available time he has to do what he loves best—taking pictures that seize the moment.

Camera-toting travelers have been in our midst ever since that magical instrument of image-making could be handheld. The photographic process was introduced in 1839 by its inventor, Louis Jacques Mandé Daguerre, a Parisian. The precursors of the first cameras were called "Daguerre boxes," unwieldy wooden contraptions, heavy and hard to carry. But that didn't stop the camera's first aficionados from roaming the streets of Paris, armed with their very own Daguerre boxes, capturing city scenes. Were Michael Clinton around in the mid-nineteenth century, he'd have been among them.

In a very real sense, the birth of photography was also the birth of travel photography. Its earliest proponents packed not only a camera but what was known as a "dark-room wagon," complete with processing chemicals. Rough roads, high winds, and hot climates were hard enough on the individual; add to this burden a bulky camera and a mobile darkroom and you can imagine how tough the going got back then.

In today's world, modern shutterbugs are far less encumbered. Cameras are smaller, lighter, often digital, and therefore not even requiring what we always believed was a concomitant essential—film. When Michael Clinton travels, he brings along two Nikons, an SLR, and a digital. There is not a trip he embarks on that doesn't include them. Even at home in New York City, he has a loaded camera at the ready—just in case there's a sunrise he can't resist or a street scene that begs to be immortalized.

GLOBAL SNAPS is a logical follow-up to his first book, **WANDERLUST**. But whereas **WANDERLUST** was a big, beautiful collection of poetically rendered travel photography, **GLOBAL SNAPS** is friendlier and more casual. Even the title is more relaxed, indeed almost nonchalant—"snaps" beings shorthand for snapshots, those informal pictures taken with a handheld camera. The word "snap" itself means "to snatch or grasp suddenly and with eagerness." And, of course, the verb "to snap" means to take a photograph.

But before jumping to conclusions about the ease with which these photos were taken, it must be said that what sounds or looks like a snap, so to speak, ain't necessarily so. It takes someone with a discerning eye, a steady hand, and sensitivity to the permutations of natural light—qualities that Clinton has in profusion. It also requires a high degree of responsiveness that comes with years of experience and an appreciation for all those images successfully captured within a nanosecond, as well as some regrets for the ones that got away.

For Michael Clinton, his photographs are his souvenirs, memories of every trip he has ever taken. Every one of them leads to a story to be told and to be treasured. Imagine more than five hundred tales—from seven different continents—based on natural and manmade wonders, wonderful people, and wondrous moments. Some are familiar, such as the Eiffel Tower in Paris; the Colosseum in Rome; and the Pyramids of Giza outside Cairo. Others are stirringly exotic—mysterious archways in Marrakech; ancient sailboats, known as *feluccas*, gracefully plying the Nile; the lunar-like landscape of Namibia in southern Africa; and the artistically sculpted glaciers of Antarctica, perhaps the last pure place on earth. There is humanity here too: the uneducated but wise-beyond-their-years natives of Bhutan, who lead their insular lives in the Himalayas; a tribe of decorous and decorated Masai natives on the Serengeti Plain; a couple in Buenos Aires, so completely and utterly focused on each other that the tango they are dancing seems as erotic as engaging in foreplay. For whimsy, there is a collection of China dolls; a passel of penguins; a selection of the strange, enchanting wildlife from the Galàpagos; and the innocent, utterly irresistible faces of children. And, of course, there are architectural details that seem like exclamation marks pointing to the heavens: church spires, minarets, and towers.

What these photographs add up to is a meticulously organized, highly personal scrapbook, the results of an intensely curious man's travels—so far. Who knows, perhaps the best is yet to come.

INTRODUCTION

My travels have taken me to more than one hundred countries and seven continents, and I have been fortunate to see so many of the world's great wonders. Whether standing at the top of Mt. Kilimanjaro in Africa after a nightlong final ascent, sleeping in the open air on an Antarctic glacier, or hiking through a remote village in Bhutan, each experience has been a moment in time that has allowed me to learn about varied ways of life—natural, architectural, cultural.

When I have stood in front of the Eiffel Tower, in Tiananmen Square, or before the Taj Mahal, it takes me a few minutes to absorb that I am actually in front of these glorious man-made wonders that have endured wars, revolutions, and natural disasters. It's the same feeling that I had as I watched the migration of the wildebeests in Tanzania's Ngorongoro Crater, stared down at the sensuous geography of Rio de Janeiro, and gazed at the grandeur of the American West. These, too, seem almost unreal to me—that I am actually there experiencing them firsthand.

In those moments, I have become enamored with places and have had experiences that live on in my memory, my photographs, and my life.

In a snap of a moment, the experience has become part of my "life lesson," and to capture that moment on film has been part of my life's goal. While I've stood in front of the Eiffel Tower at least forty times, each time has had its own moment of distinction. The seasons, the light, the grounds—all have created the backdrop for a unique experience. I've spent romantic moments, family moments, work moments, and solitary moments there. I've stood on the Champs de Mars, in black tie, watching a fireworks display to the music of *An American in Paris*; I've dined in the Restaurant Jules Verne, and I've eaten cheese sandwiches on a park bench below the tower's majestic spire. And I have tried to photograph many of these different moments—whether at dawn, midday, or at night—to snap a particular moment in time.

Each snap has been my own moment of experience that conjures up emotions of happiness, awe, loss, and sadness. And I've had to try to separate the many different moments from each other, as they all blend into that one, overall "Eiffel Tower" experience.

I'm sure that you, too, can step back and think about your own moment in front of a place you have dreamed about visiting. It may have been after acting on a life-time dream to visit this place; or it may have been through circumstances that led you there. Regardless, just close your eyes for a second and you can re-create that snap of a moment and what it ultimately meant to you.

For me, having a long list of these moments is more important than what material goods I might accumulate over my lifetime. It's the sum of a lifetime of traveling the globe that is my life's quest.

GLOBAL SNAPS is a selection of several hundred photos from the seven continents—my captured moments that recollect people, places, natural wonders, and man-made marvels. This is not a comprehensive view of the world in its entirety, it's a highly personal collection of photographs of the places I have been drawn to visit. I am hopeful, nonetheless, that these photographs will inspire every reader to create his or her own wide-ranging snaps through travel, or that they will offer transport to places you might never actually go yourself but can visit through my eyes. This book is a very personal approach, although the cache of photographs is huge. This is a comprehensive look at the world; but it's *my* comprehensive look, so don't expect to see everything in an encyclopedic format. Just expect that what you do see here will be what has inspired and encouraged me. I hope that it will inspire and encourage you, too.

MICHAEL CLINTON
NEW YORK

II

Jaipur, India

12

ANTARCTICA

ANTARCTICA

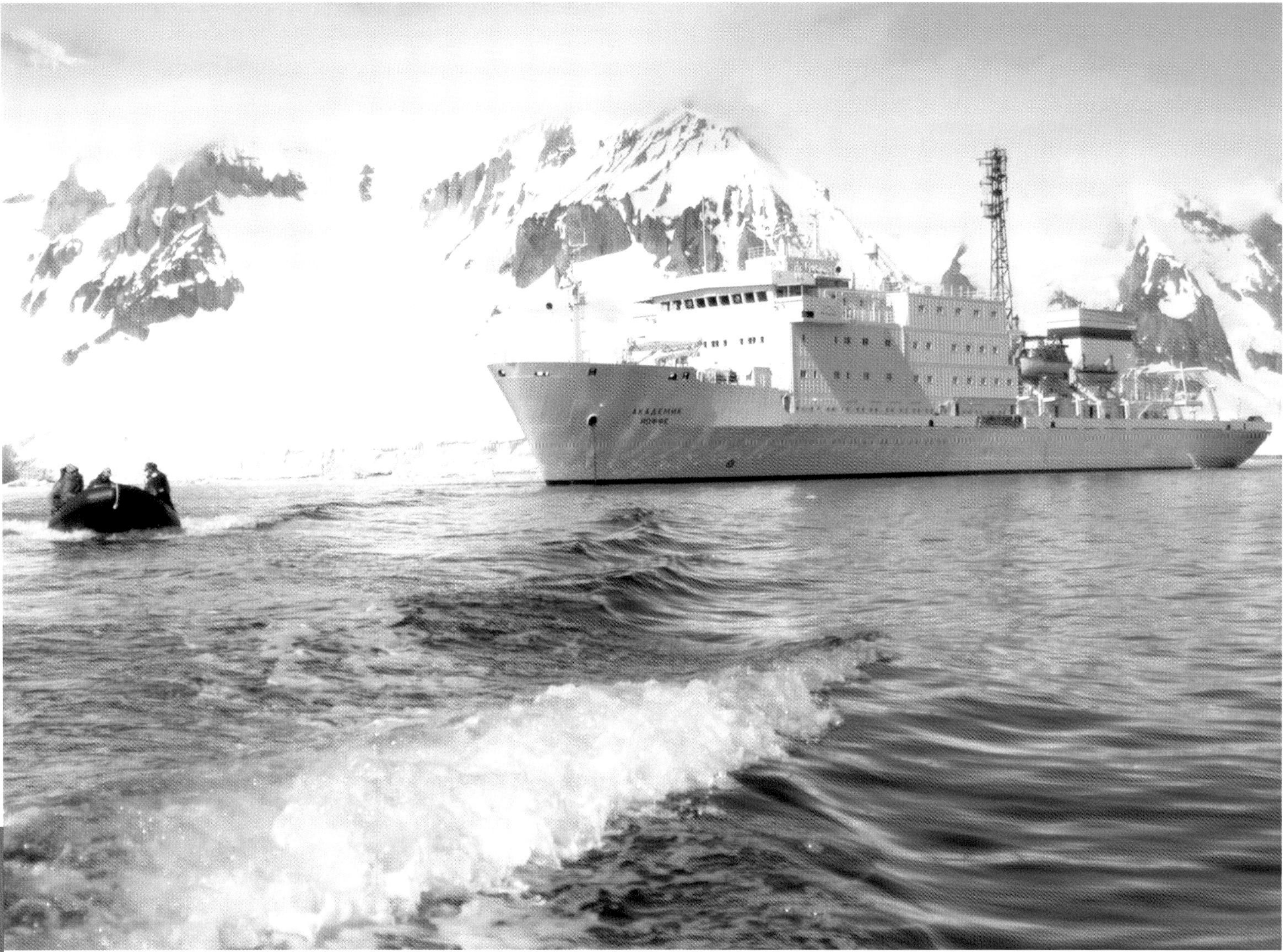
АКАДЕМИК
ИОФФЕ

The author celebrates traveling to his 100th country. Photo by Todd Marsh.

8.5×3.05×12-66 MEN
AKADEMIK IOFFE
KALININGRAD

26

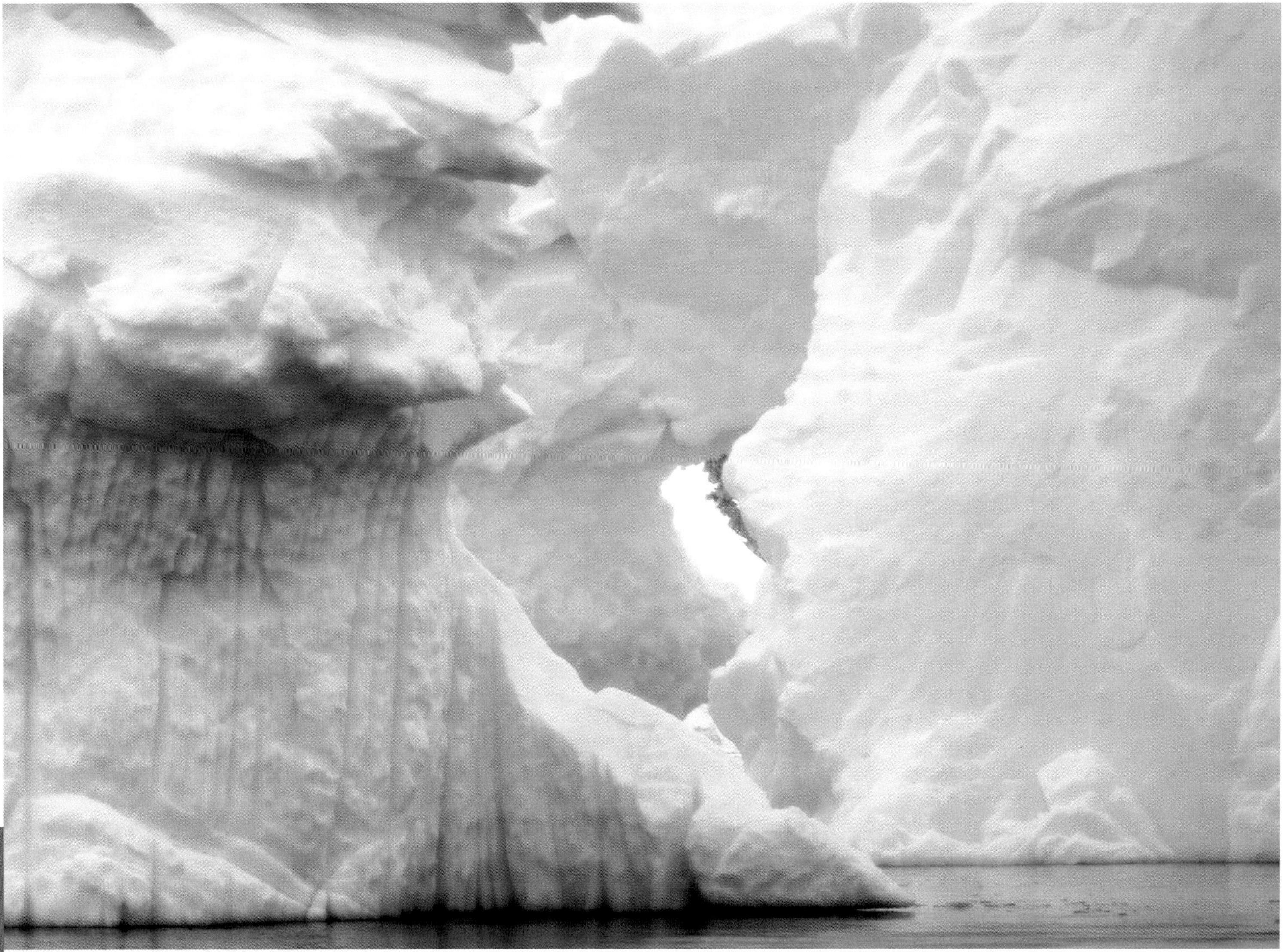

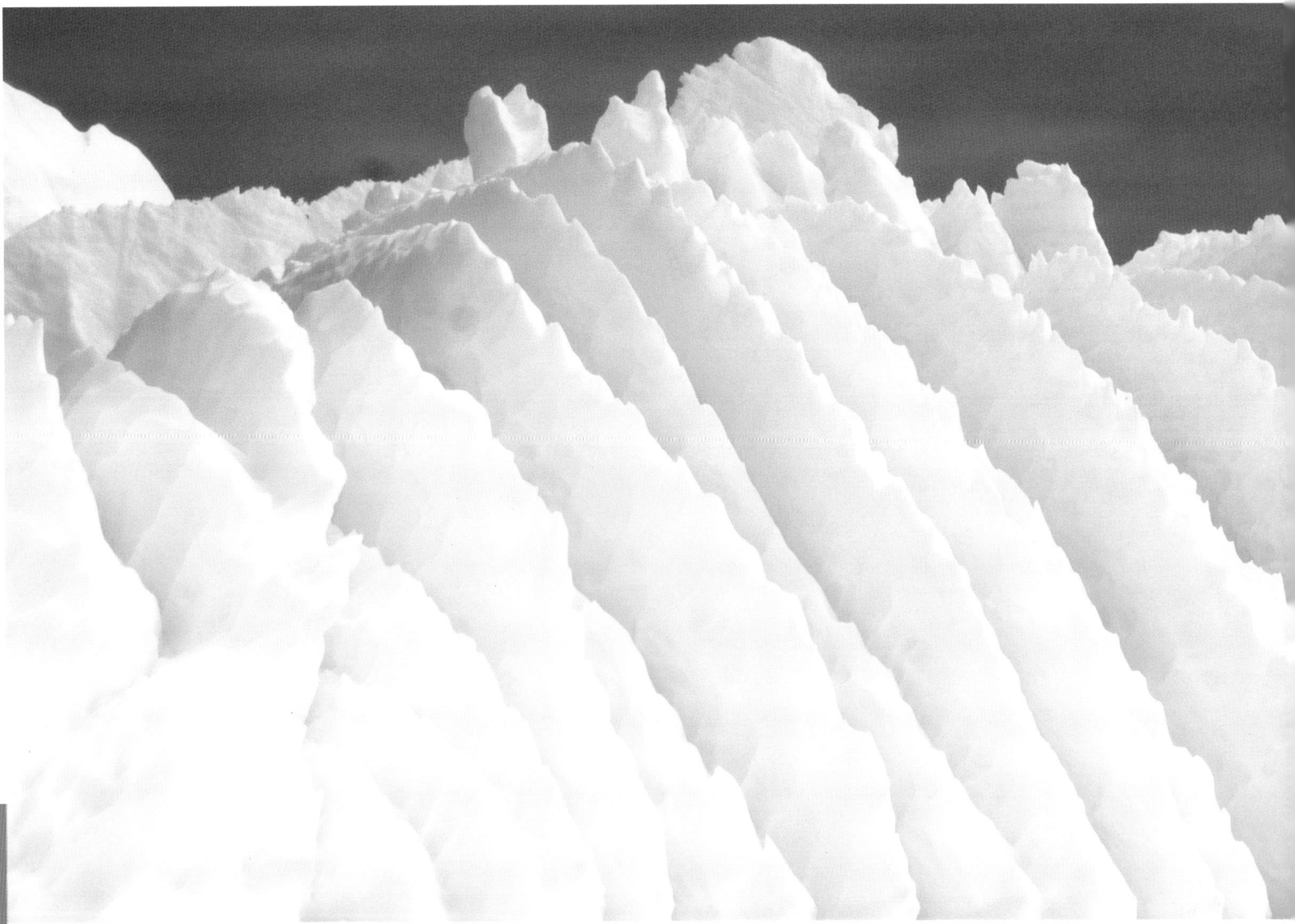

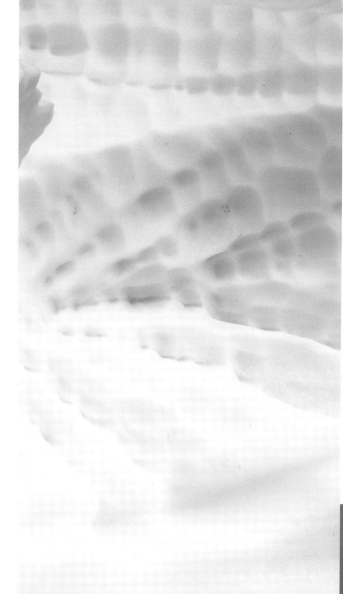

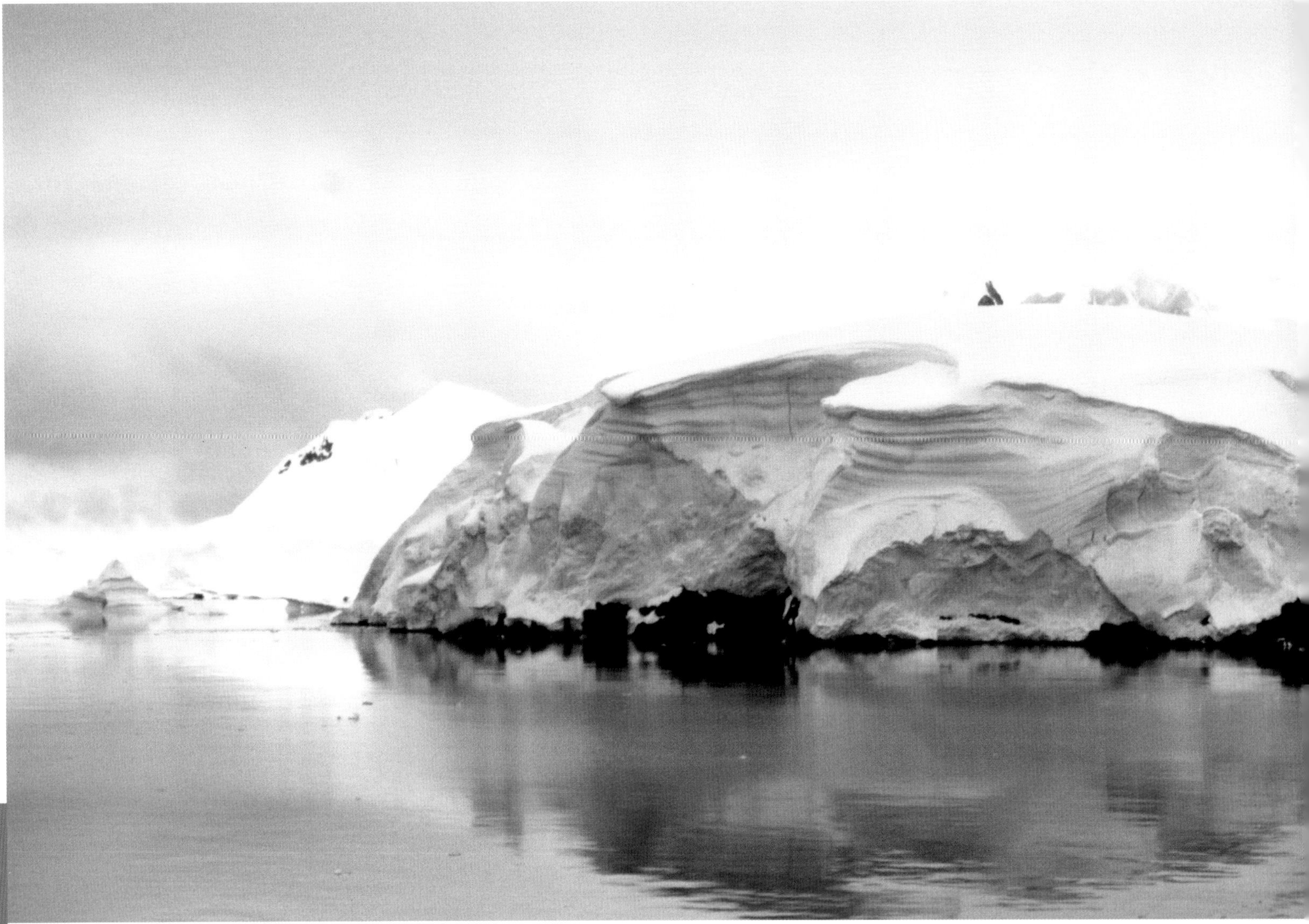

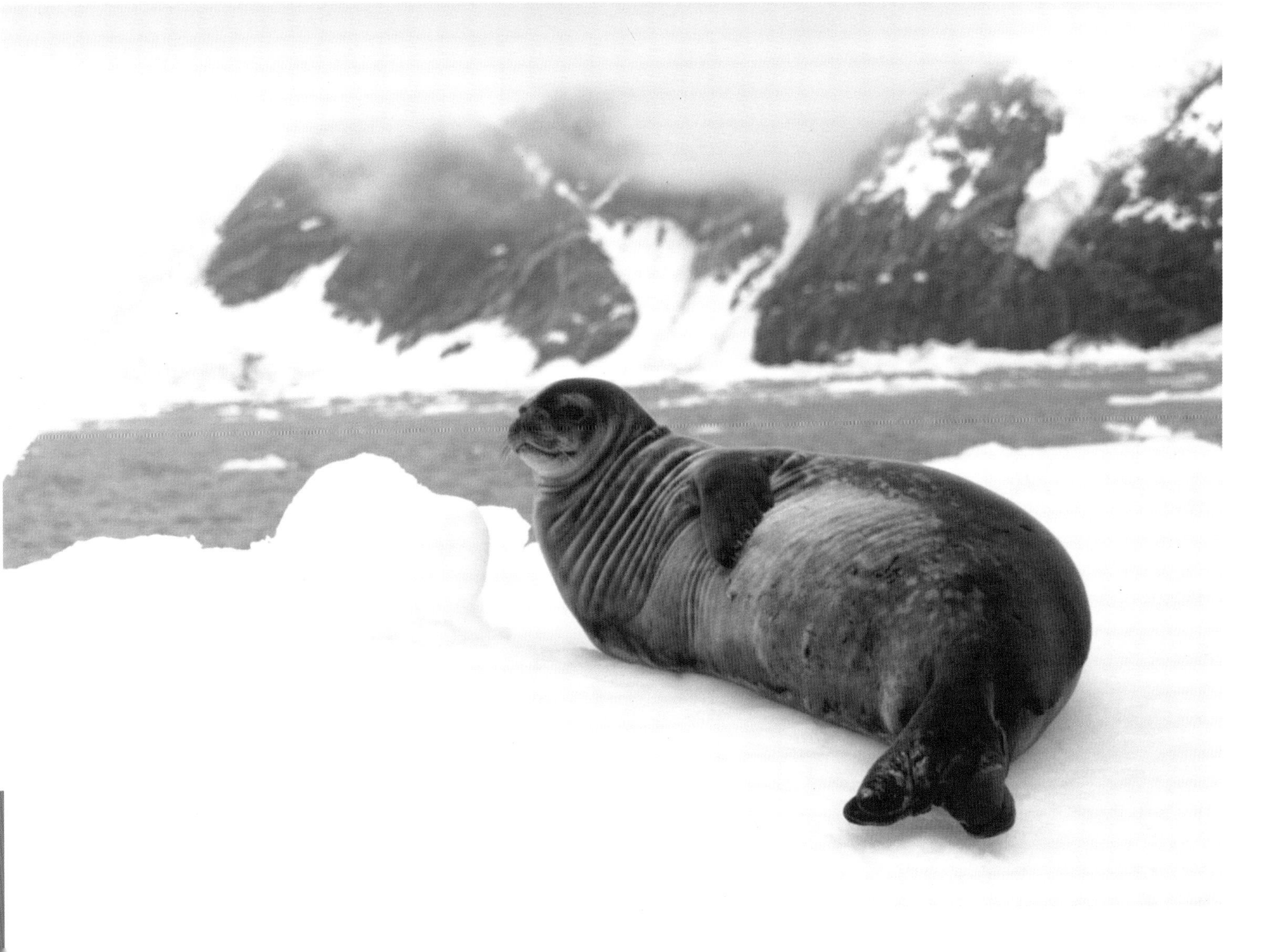

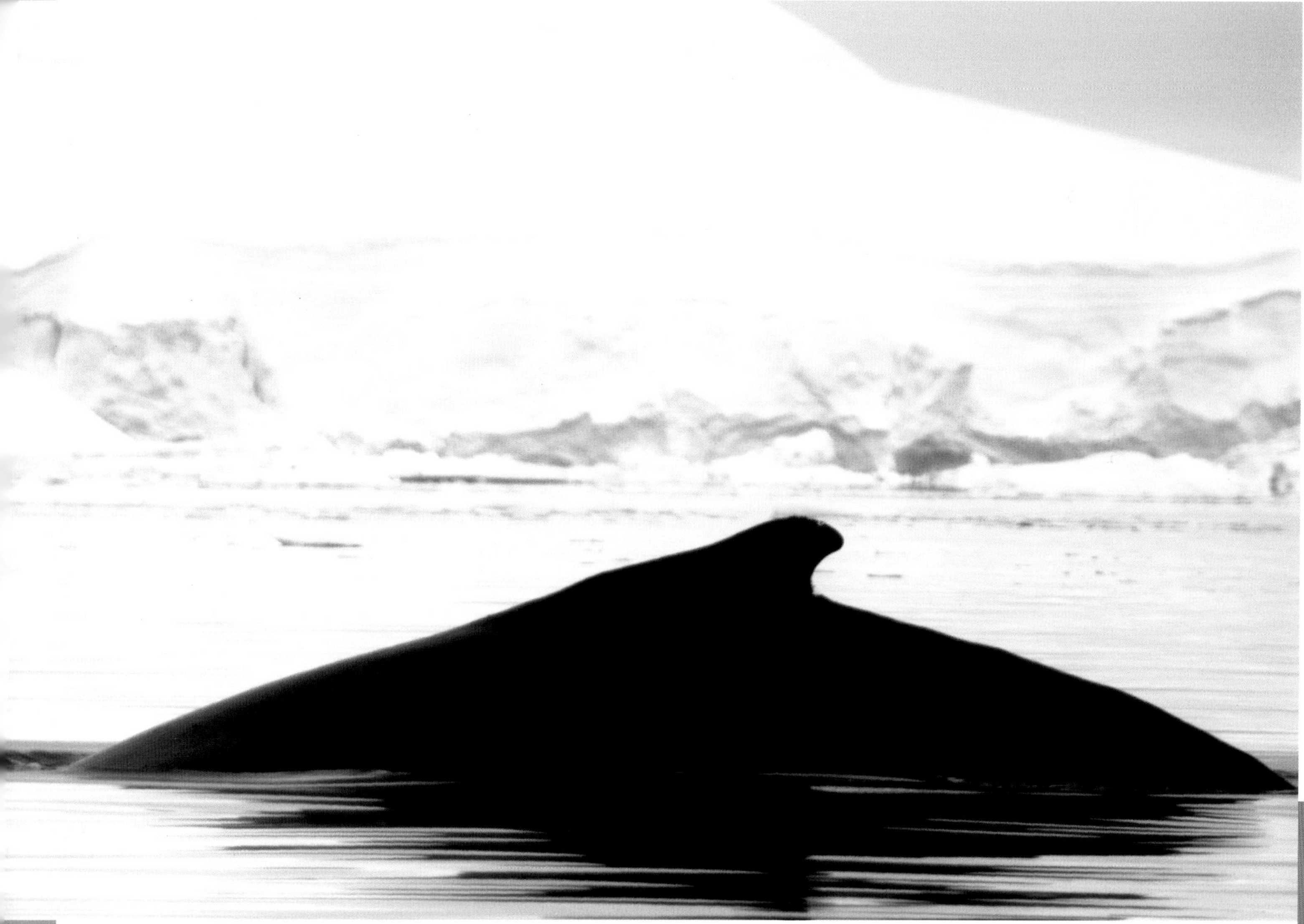

48

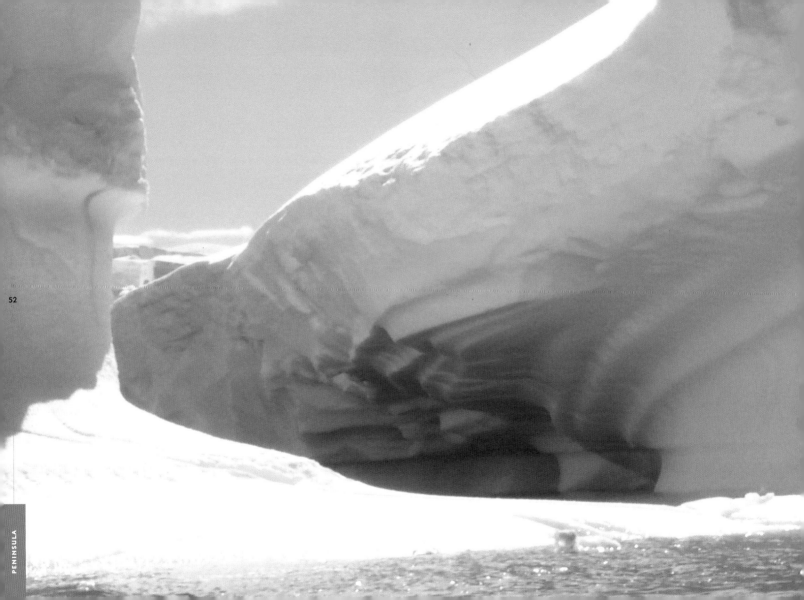

SOUTH AMERICA

Argentina
Bolivia
Brazil
Chile
Colombia
Ecuador
Guyana
Paraguay
Peru
Suriname
Uruguay
Venezuela

SOUTH AMERICA

ARGENTINA

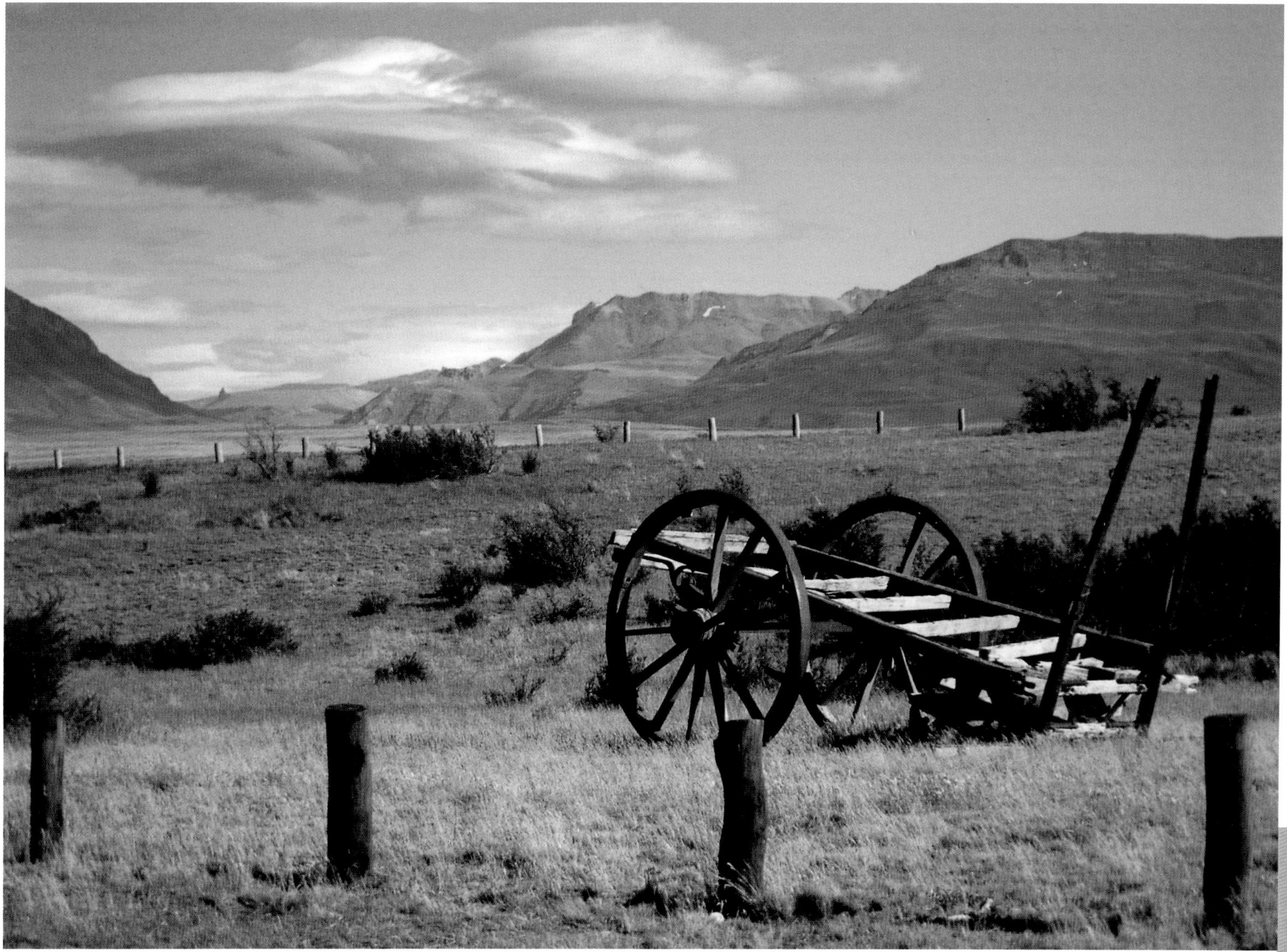

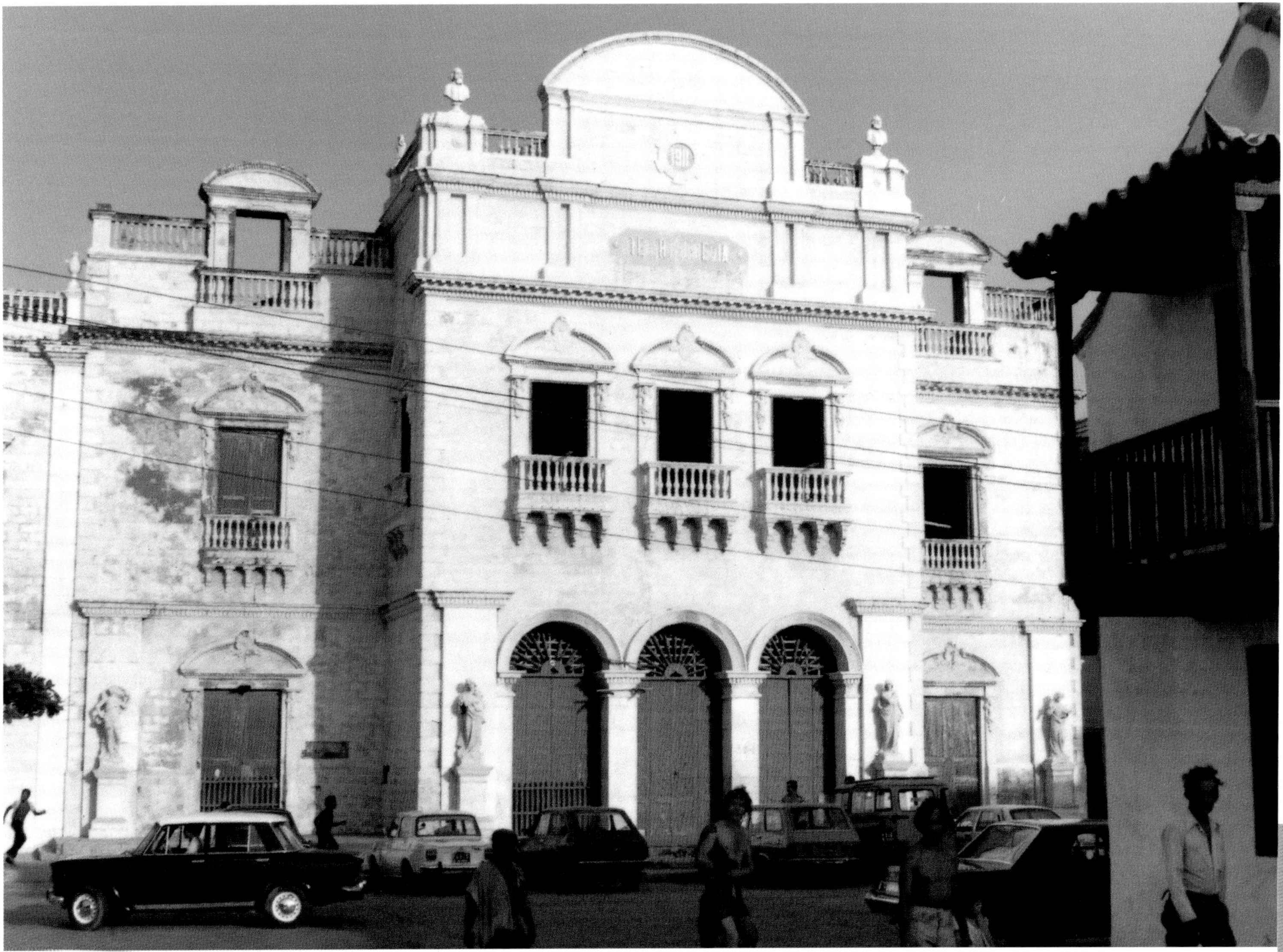

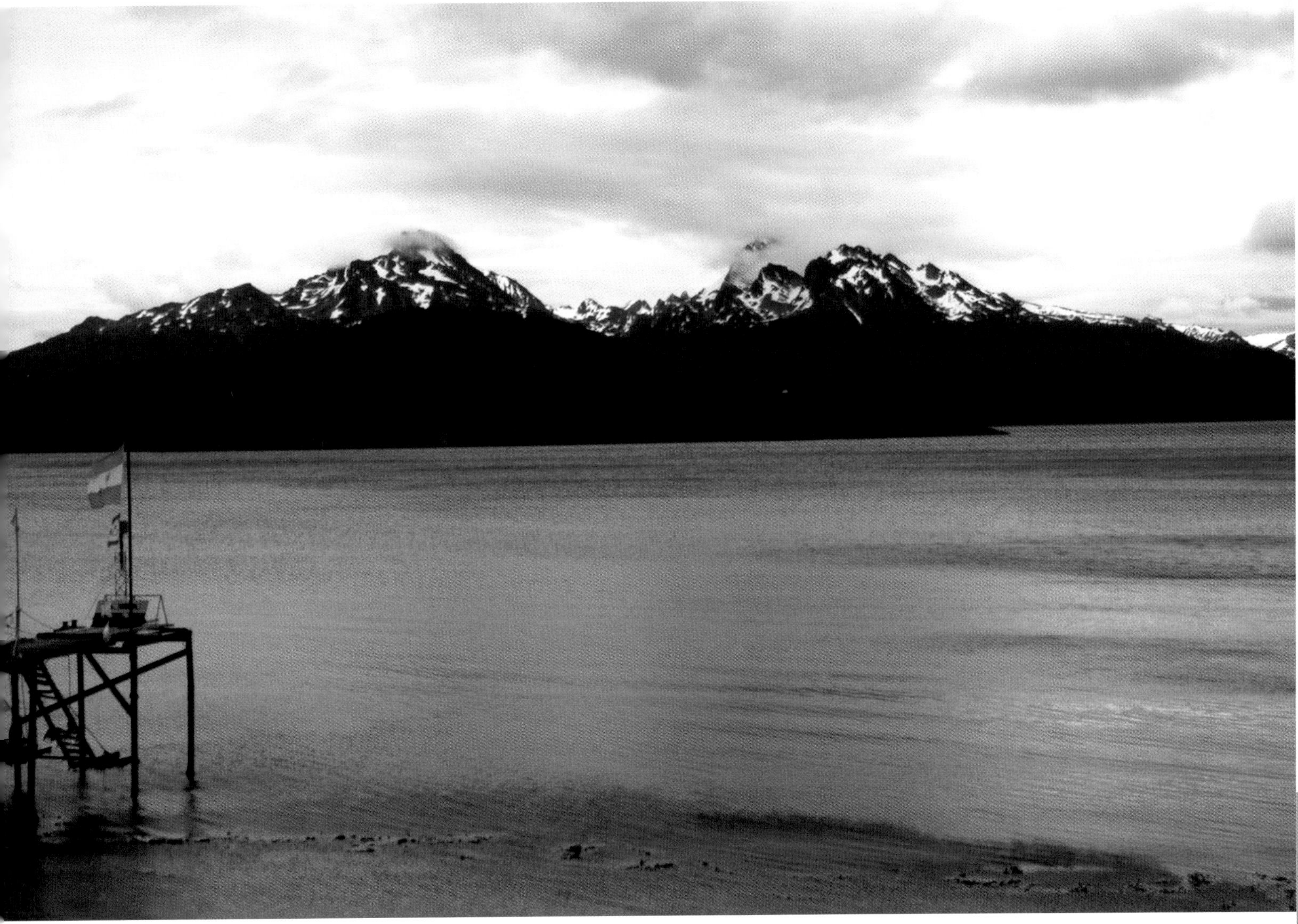

64

~ PELIGRO ~ NO PASAR ~

Los desprendimientos de hielo
producen astillas que son
arrojadas con violencia a
varias decenas de metros.
Entre 1968 y 1988, 32 personas
murieron por esta causa.

When ice falls, pieces
are thrown violently
dozens of meters away.
This action produced
the death of 32 people
between 1968 and 1988.

· DANGER ~ NO TRESPASSING ·

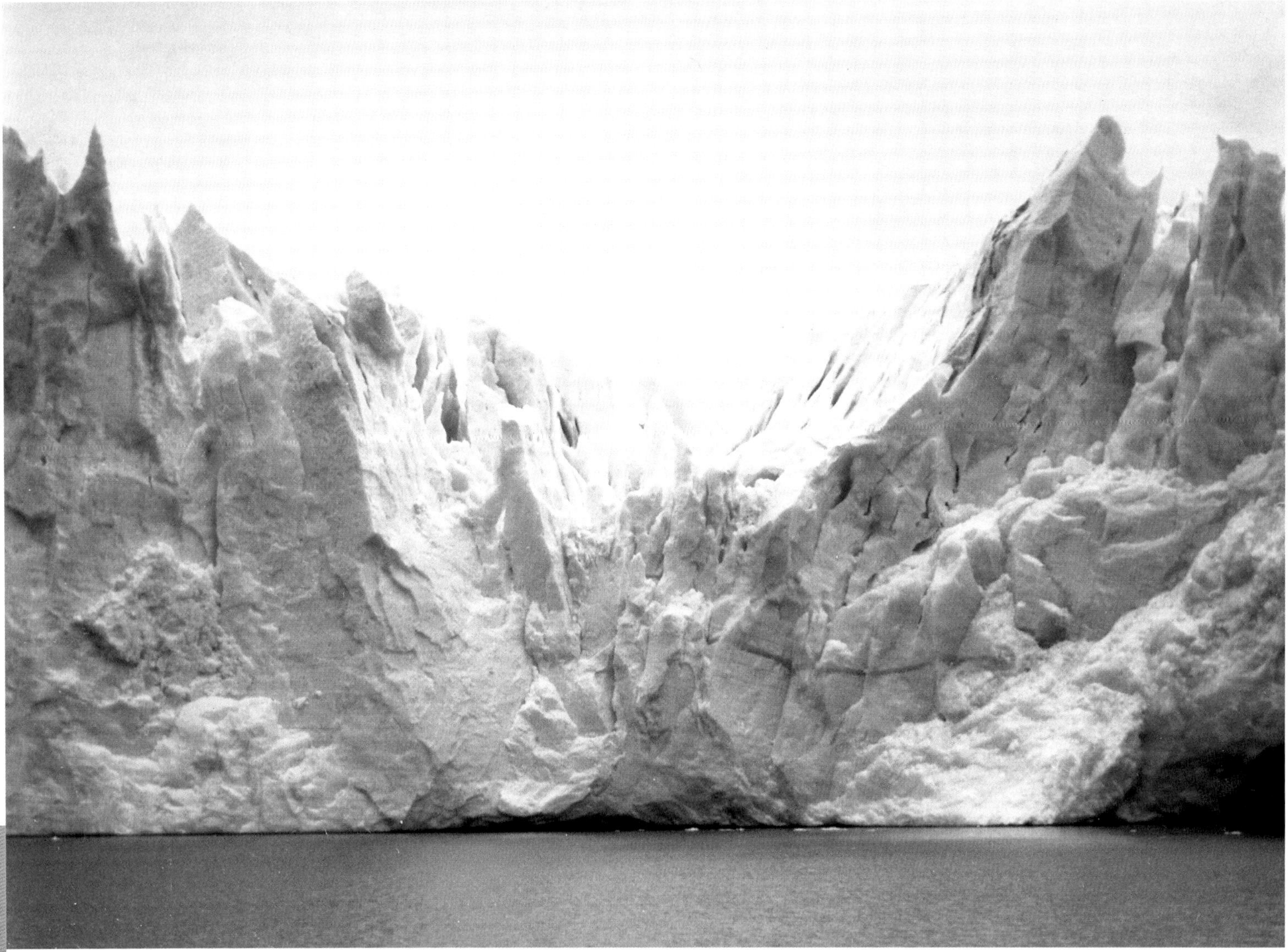

BOLIVIA

COLOMBIA

ECUADOR

PERU

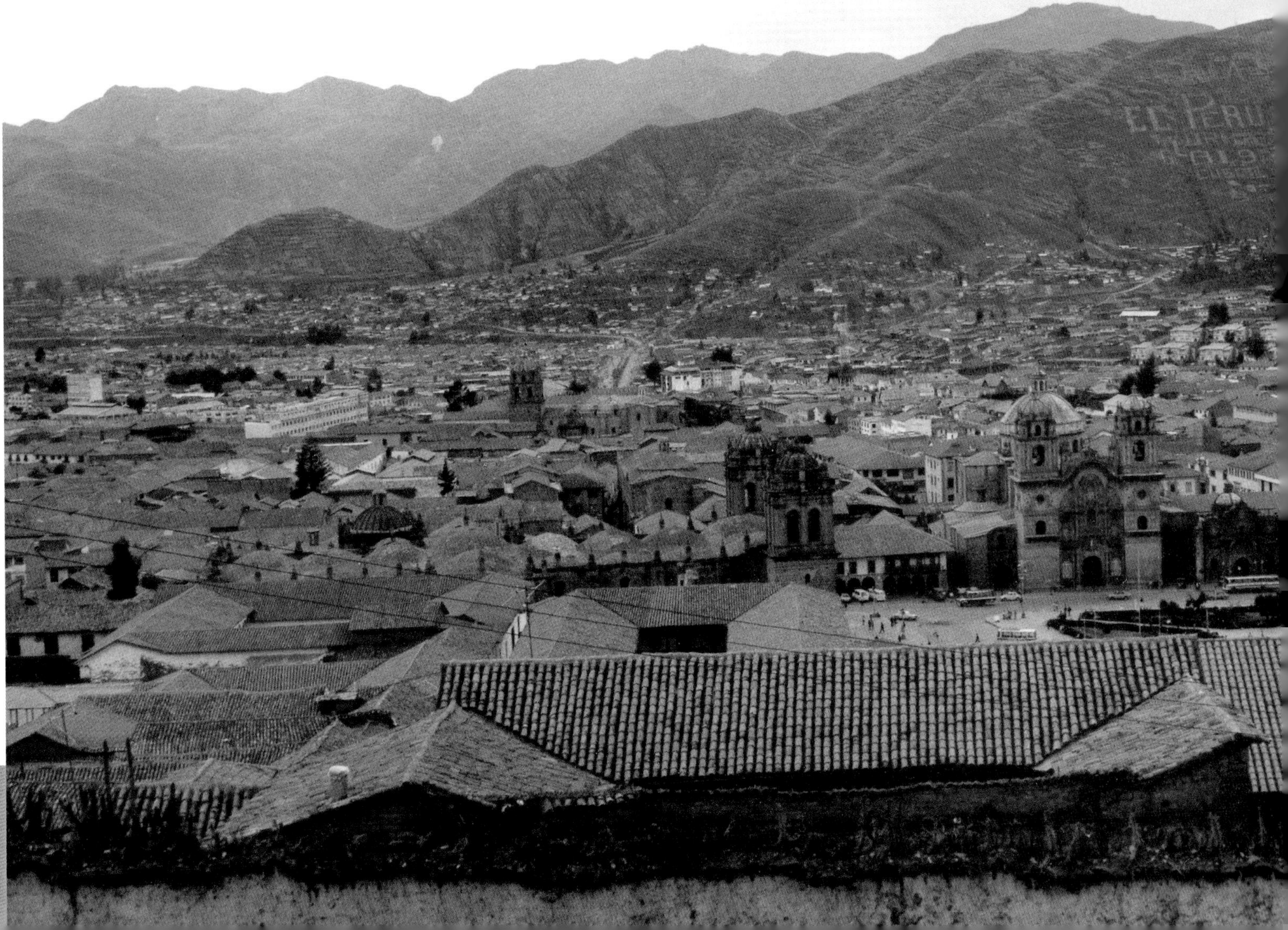

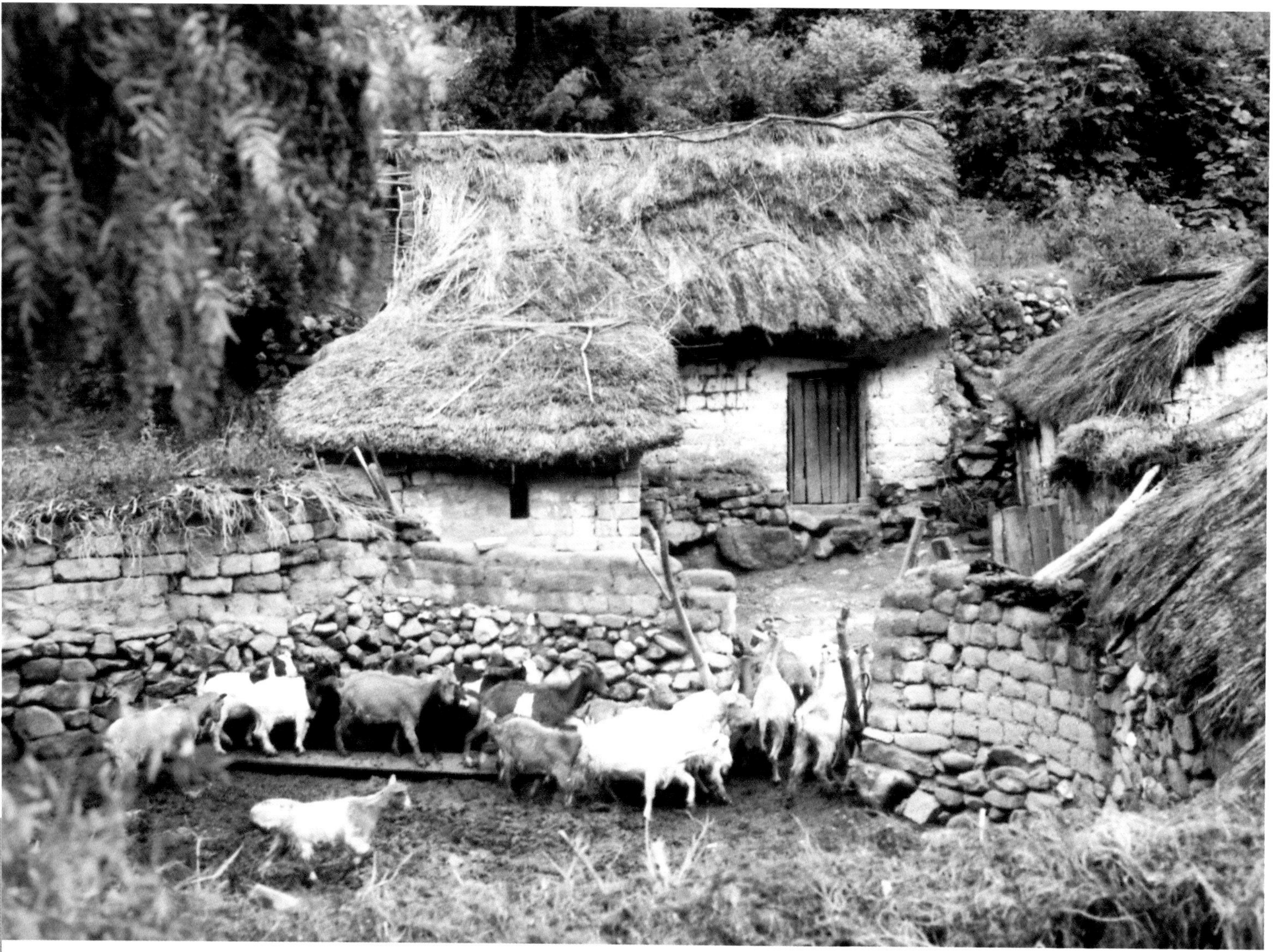

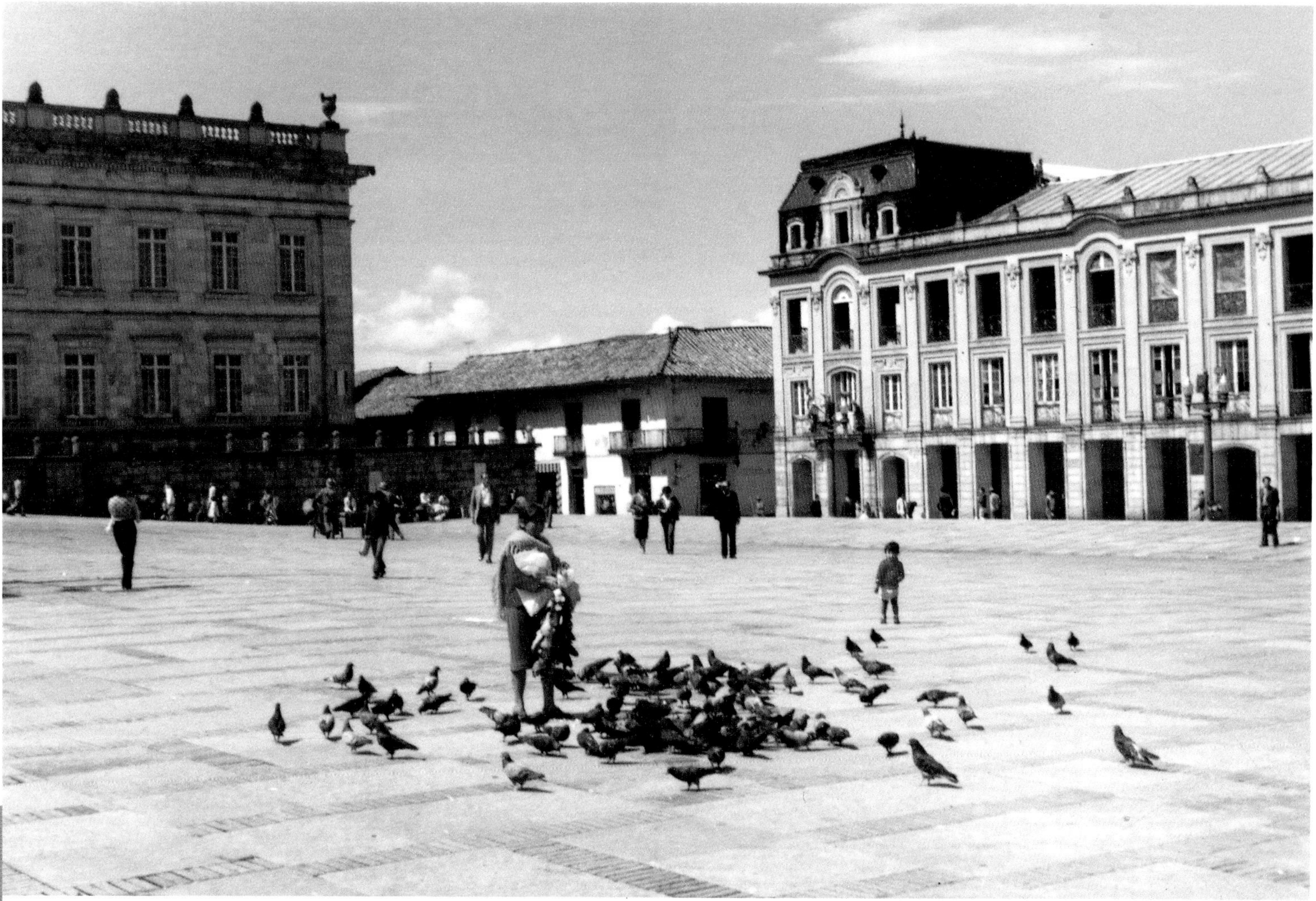

NORTH AMERICA

Anguilla	Haiti
Antigua & Barbuda	Honduras
Bahamas	Jamaica
Barbados	Mexico
Belize	Nicaragua
Canada	Panama
Costa Rica	St. Kitts & Nevis
Cuba	St. Lucia
Dominica	St. Vincent &
Dominican Rep.	the Grenadines
El Salvador	Trinidad & Tobago
Grenada	United States
Guatemala	

NORTH AMERICA

ANGUILLA

92

COSTA RICA

The author in the rain forest. Photo by Tom DeVincentis.

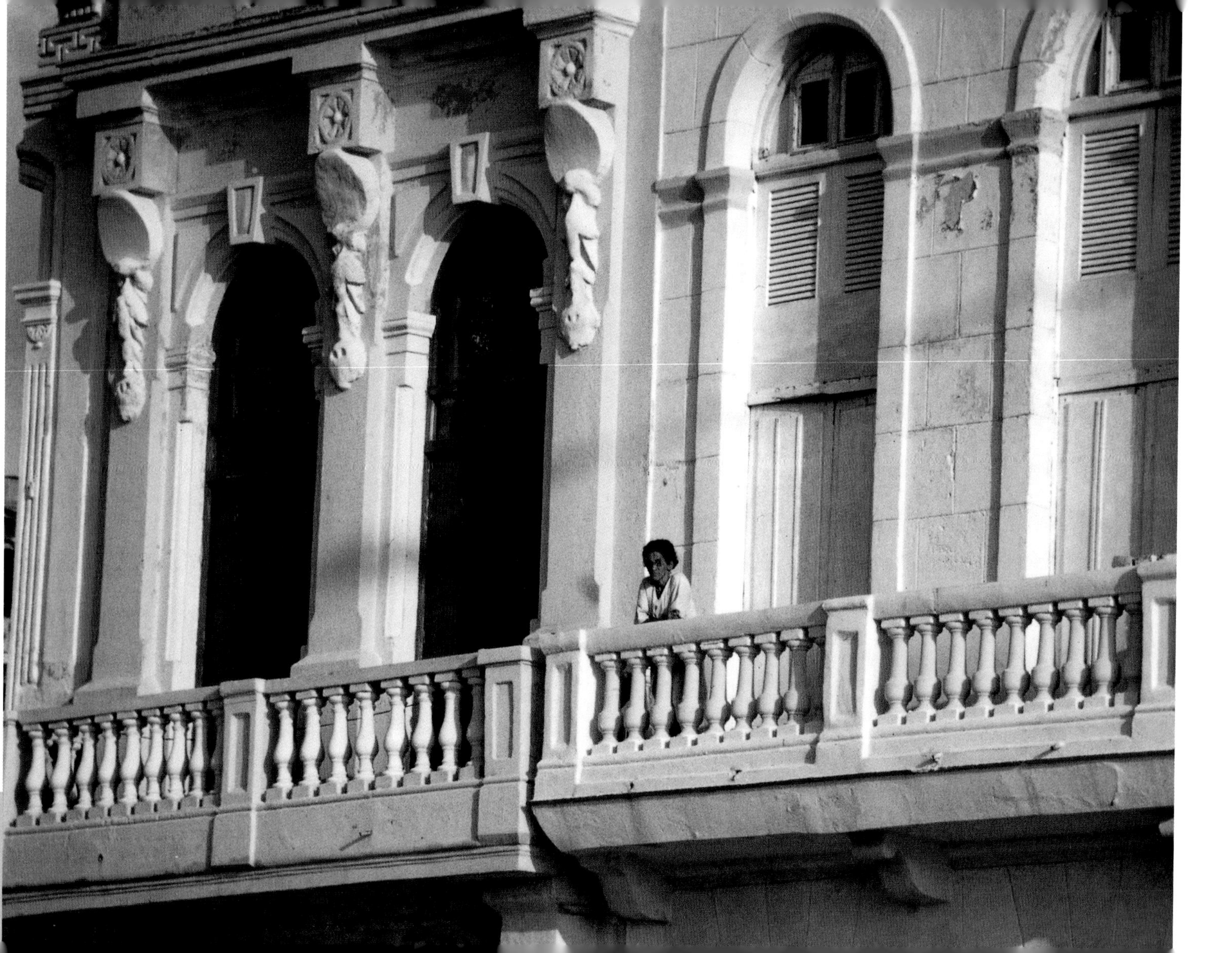

CUBA

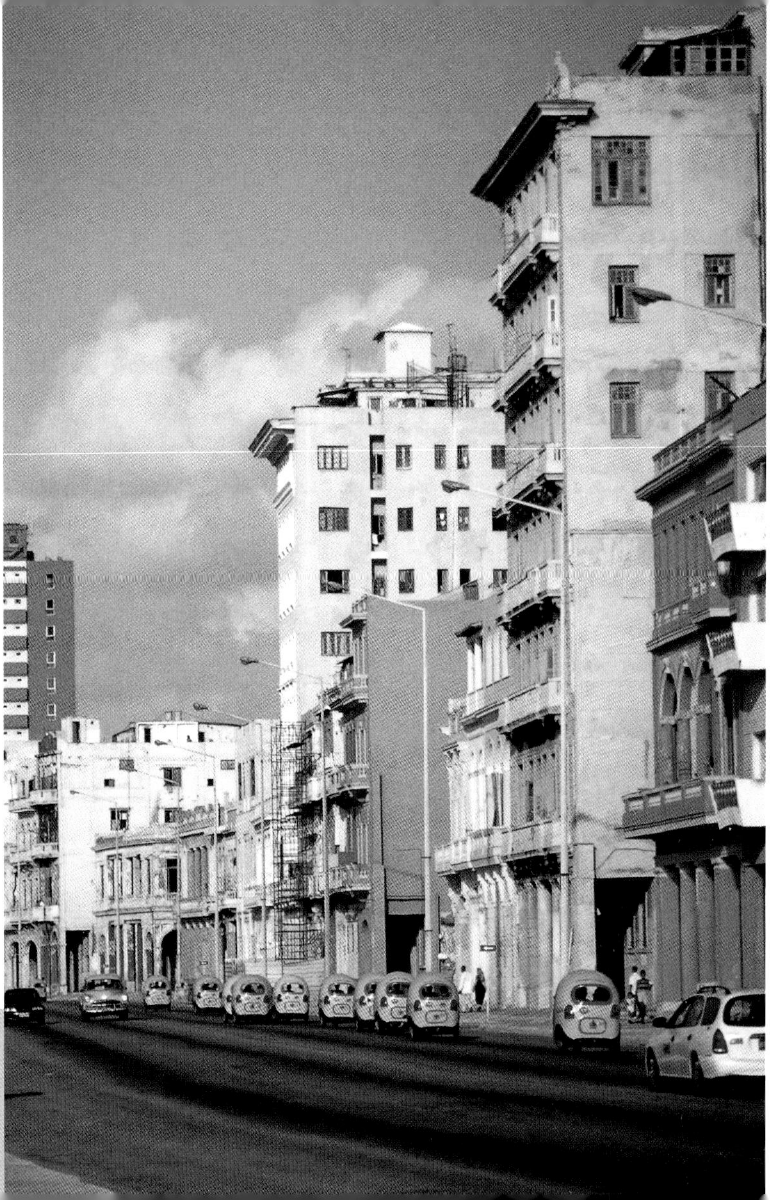

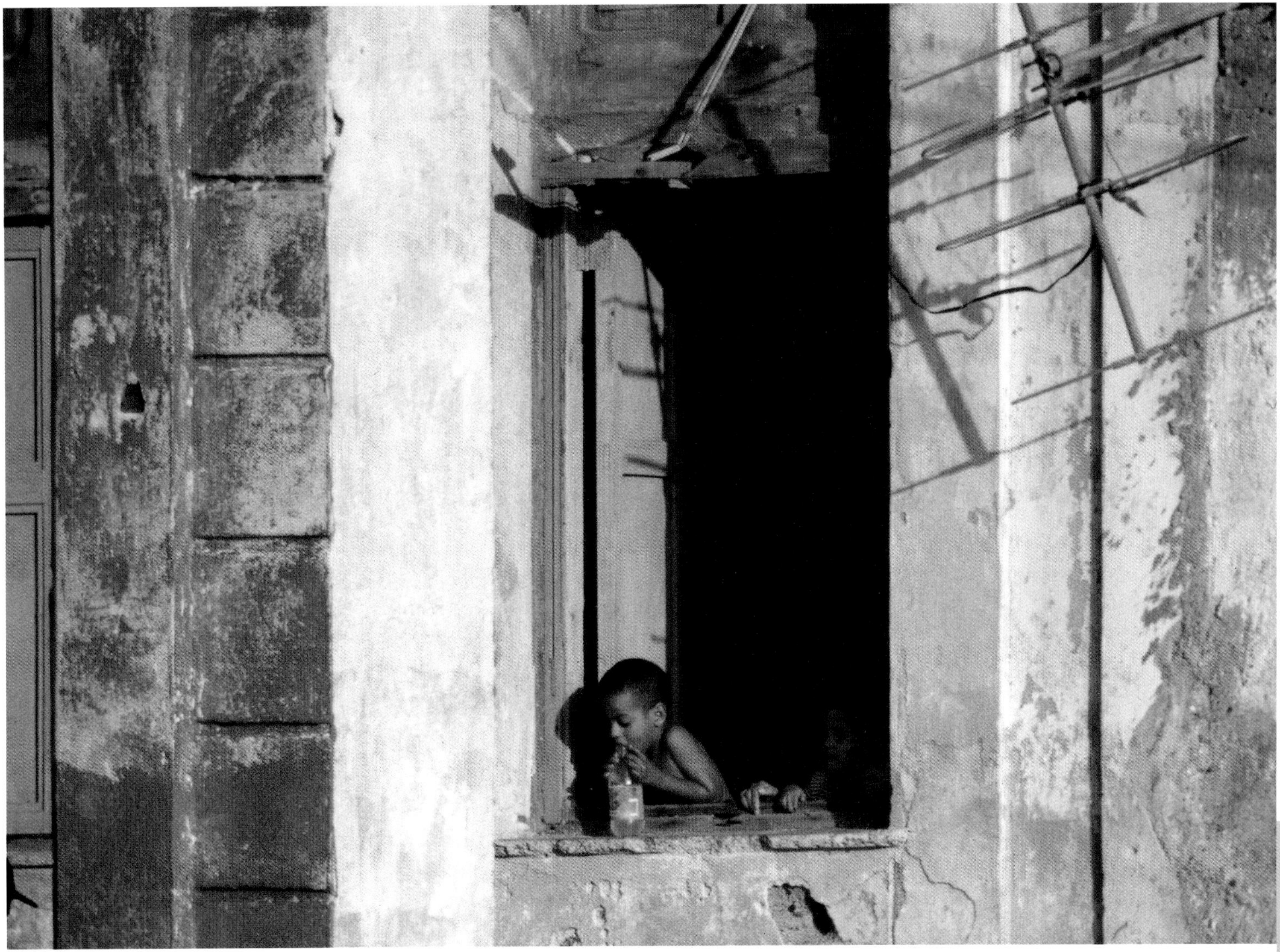

MEXICO

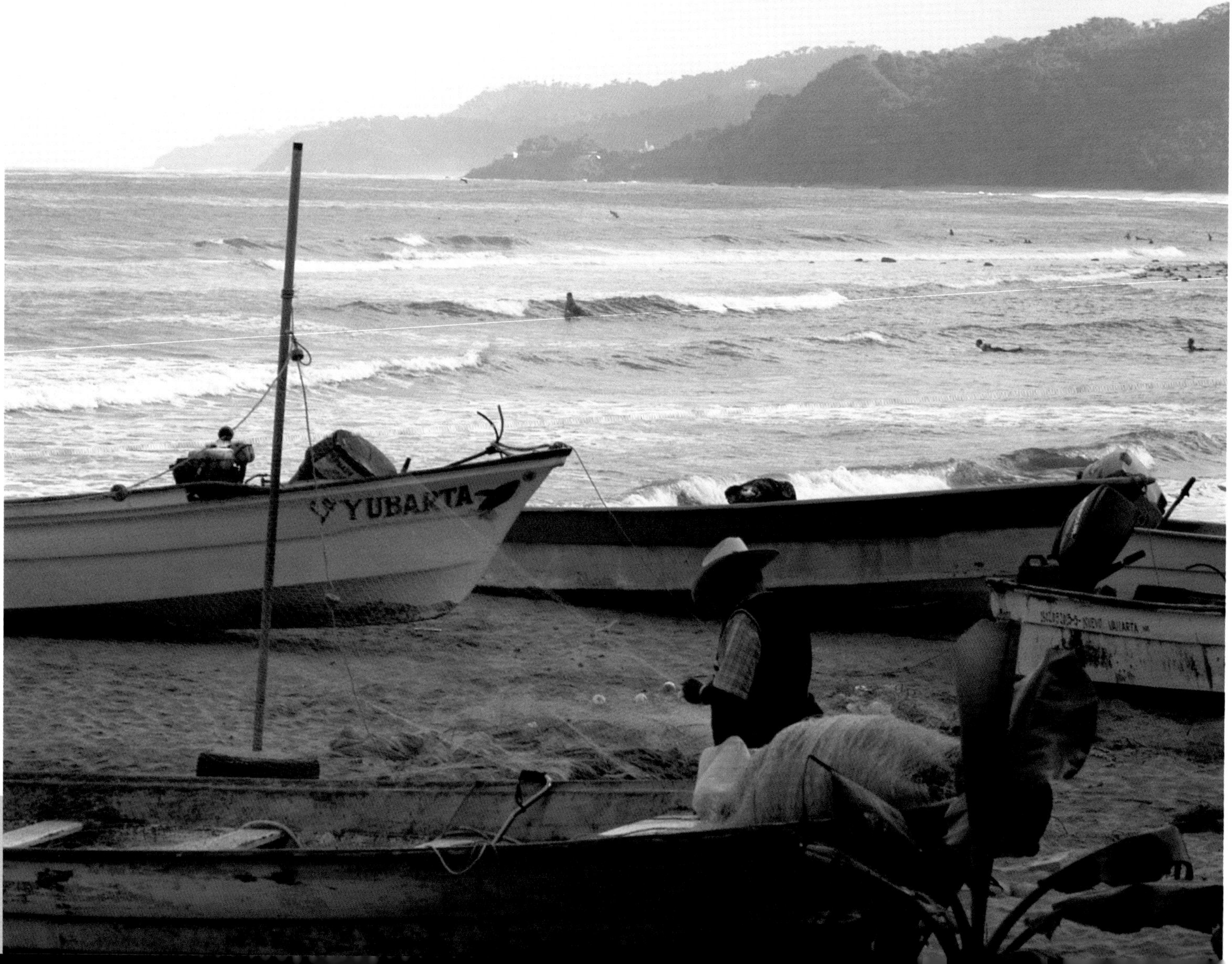
YUBARTA

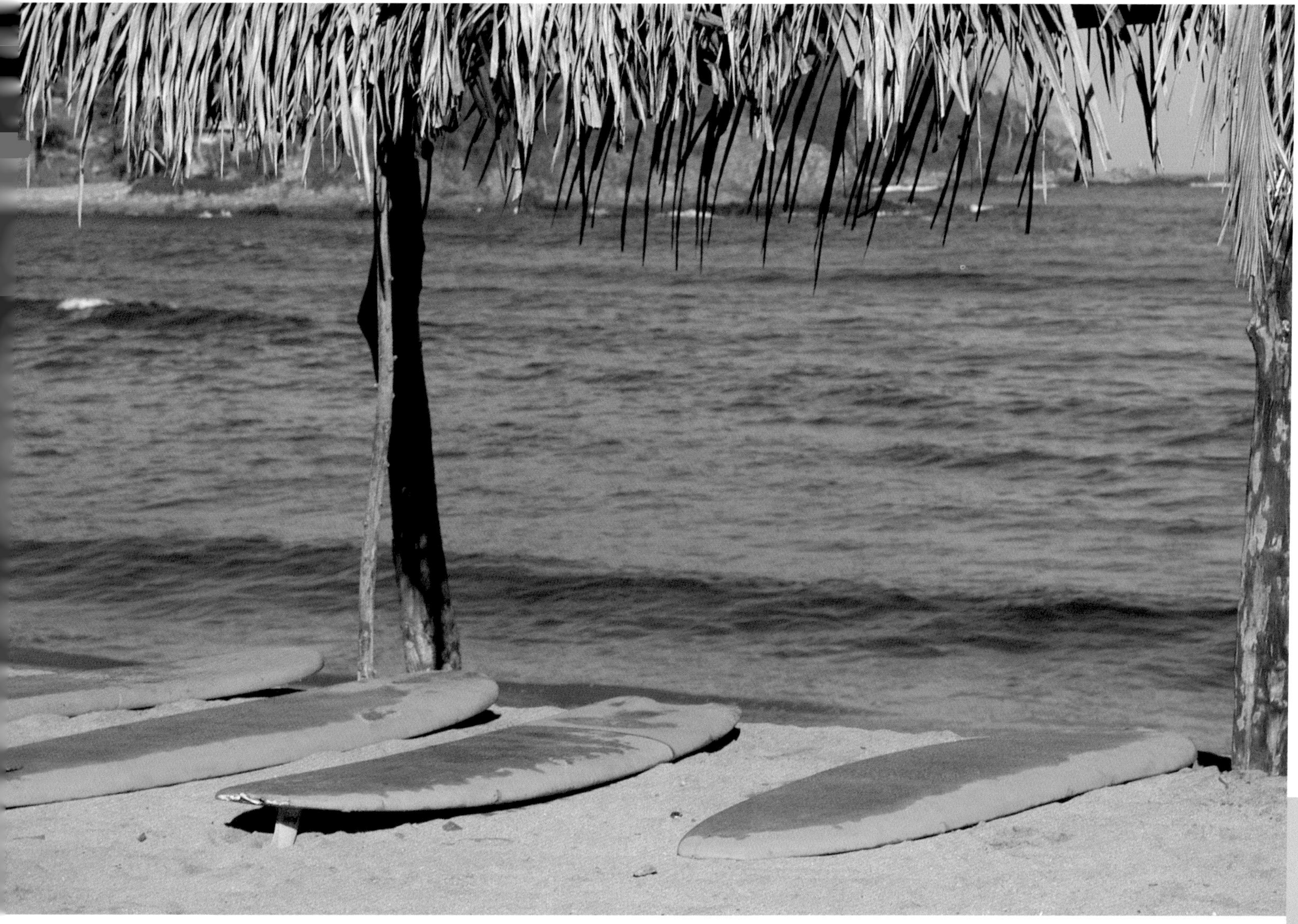

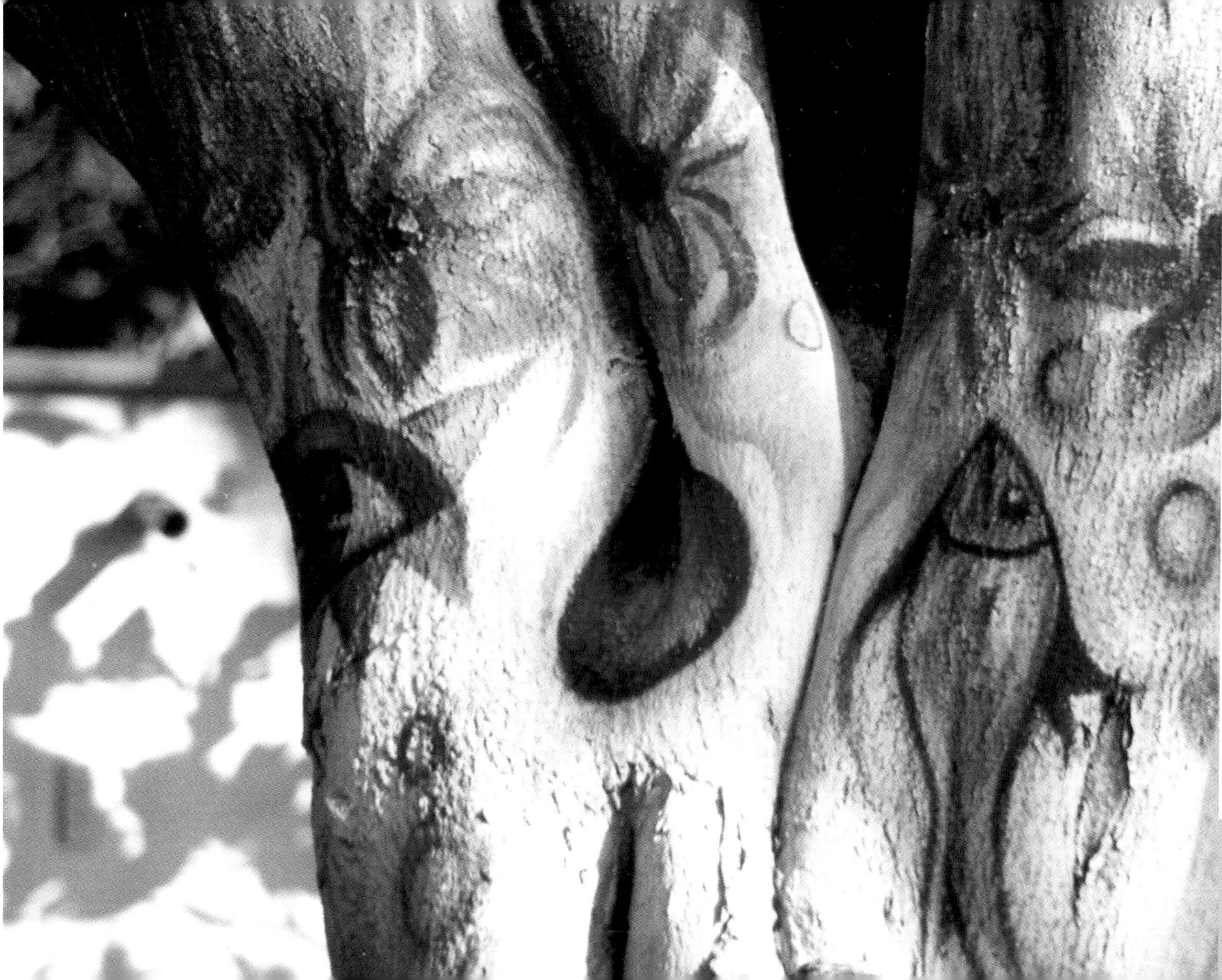

UNITED STATES

118

SACRED MONUMENT
TRAIL RIDES

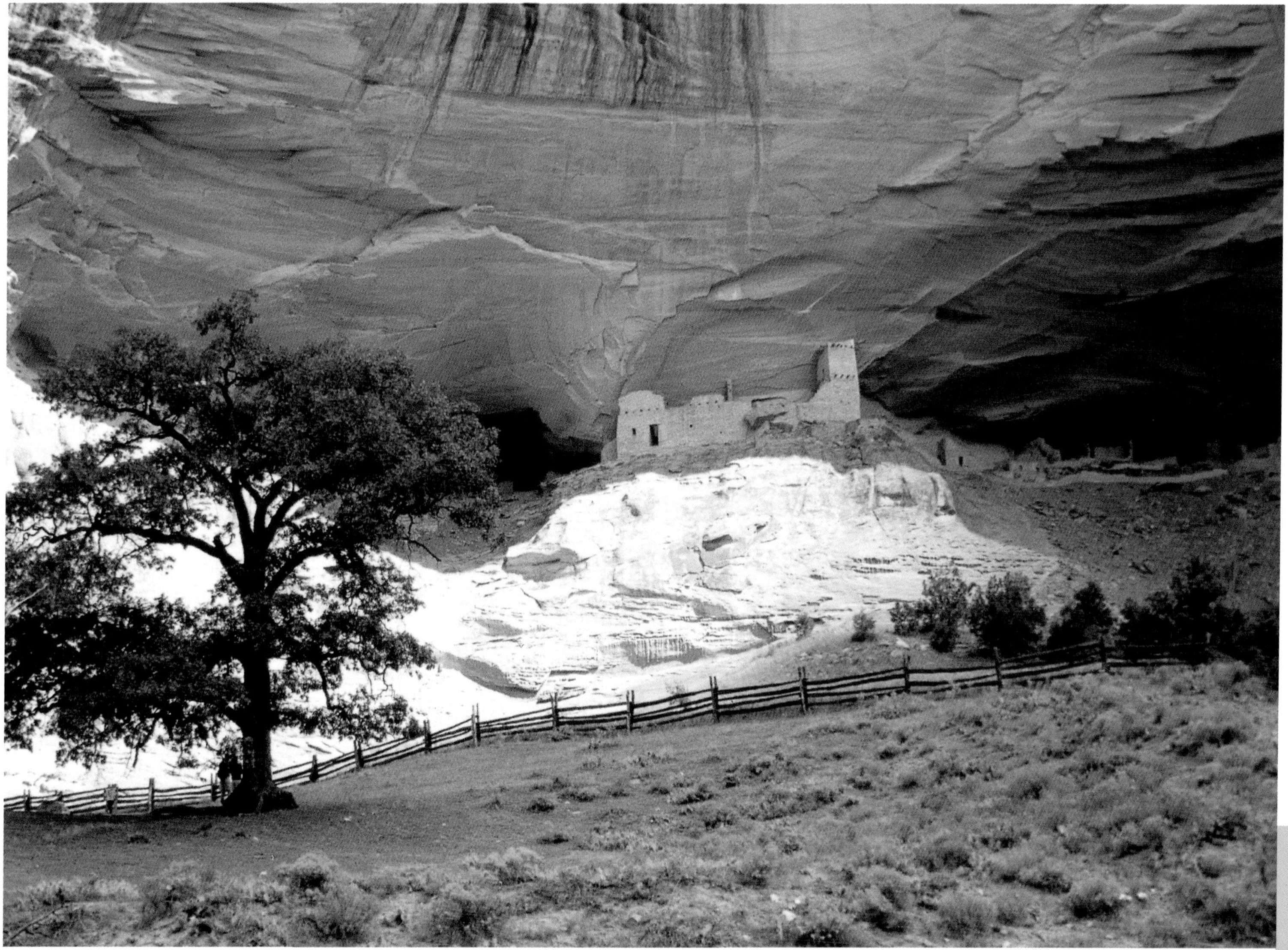

124

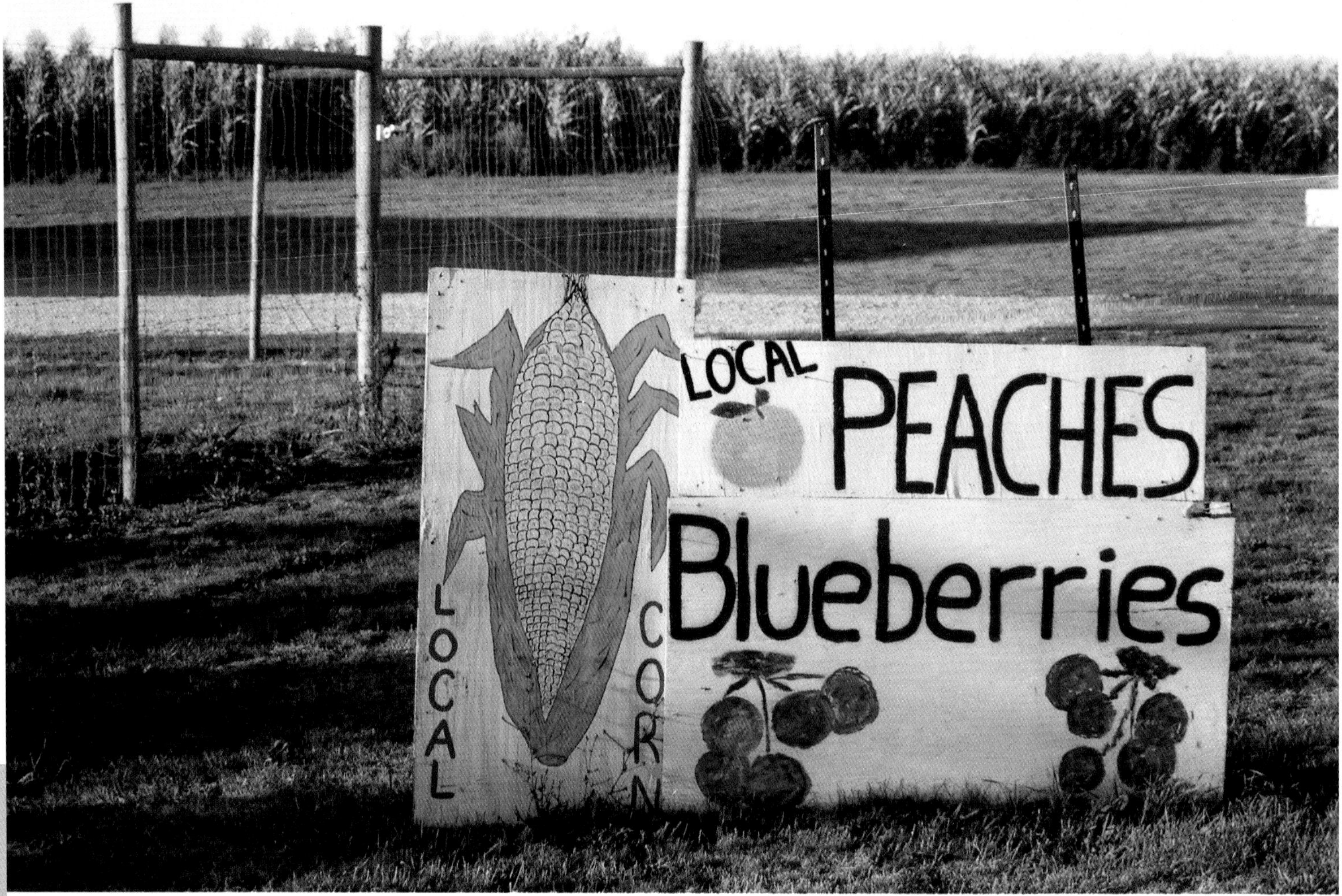
LOCAL
PEACHES
Blueberries
LOCAL
CORN

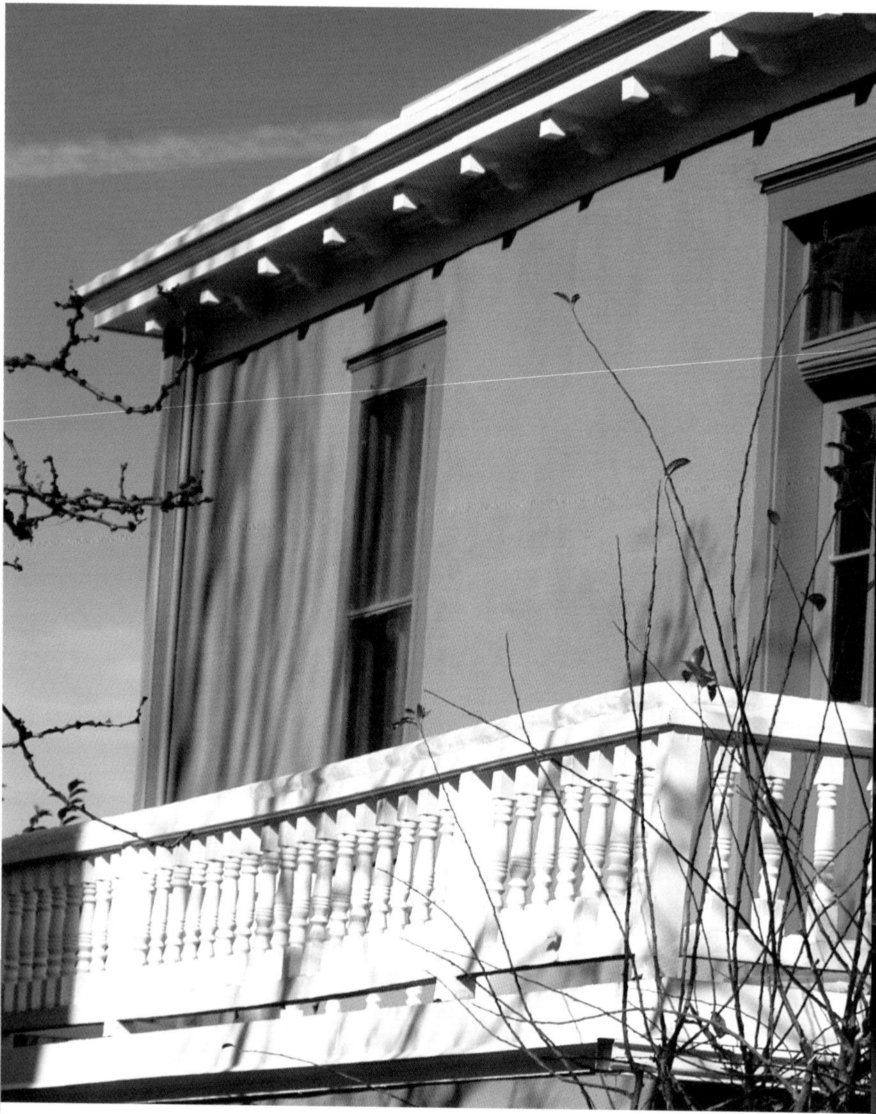

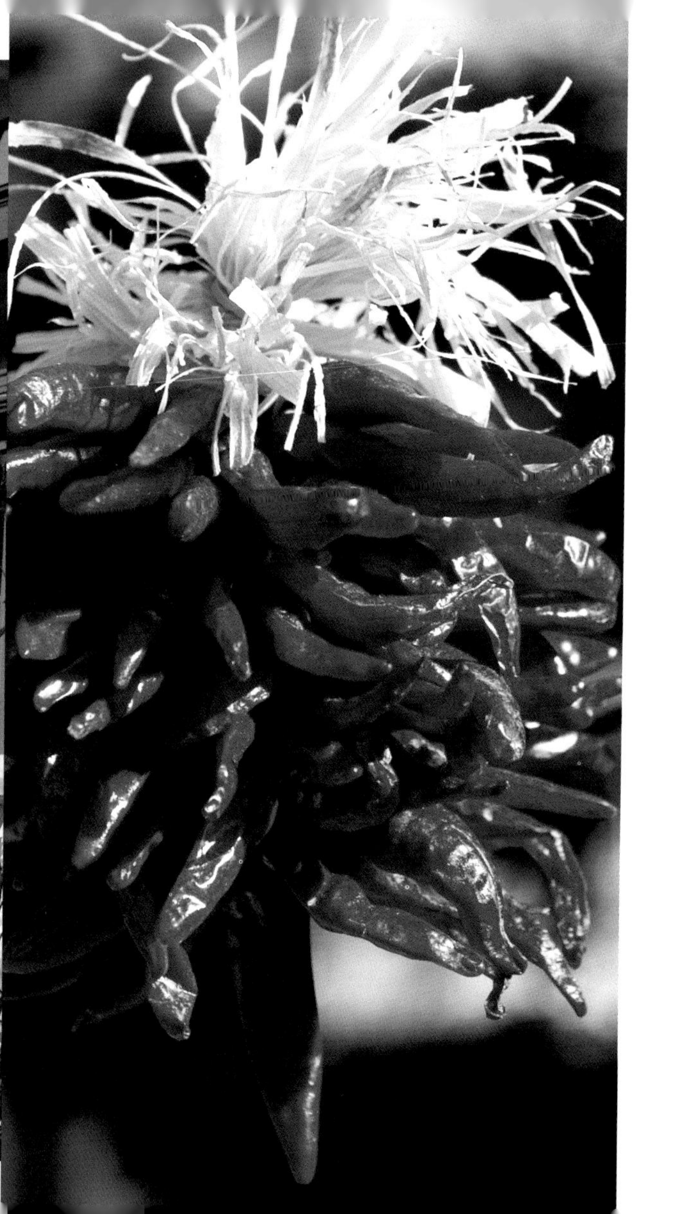

131

SANTA FE

BIENVILLE

ONE WAY

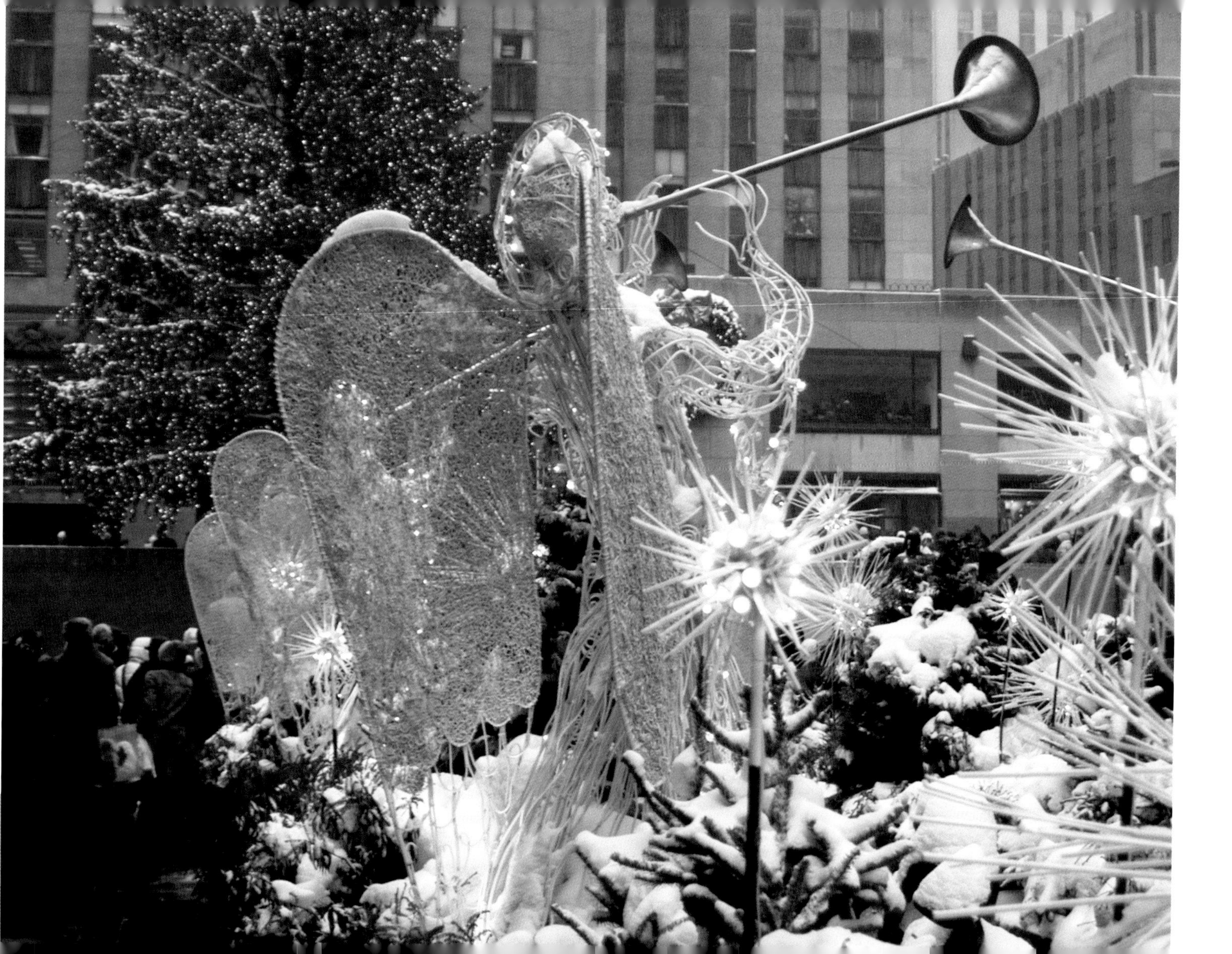

EUROPE

Albania	Greece	Serbia &
Andorra	Hungary	Montenegro
Armenia	Iceland	(Yugoslavia)
Austria	Ireland	Slovakia
Azerbaijan	Italy	Slovenia
Belarus	Latvia	Spain
Belgium	Liechtenstein	Sweden
Bosnia &	Lithuania	Switzerland
Herzegovina	Luxembourg	Turkey
Bulgaria	Macedonia	Ukraine
Croatia	Malta	United Kingdom
Cyprus	Moldova	Vatican City
Czech Republic	Monaco	
Denmark	Netherlands	
Estonia	Norway	
Finland	Poland	
France	Portugal	
Georgia	Romania	
Germany	San Marino	

EUROPE

CROATIA

DENMARK

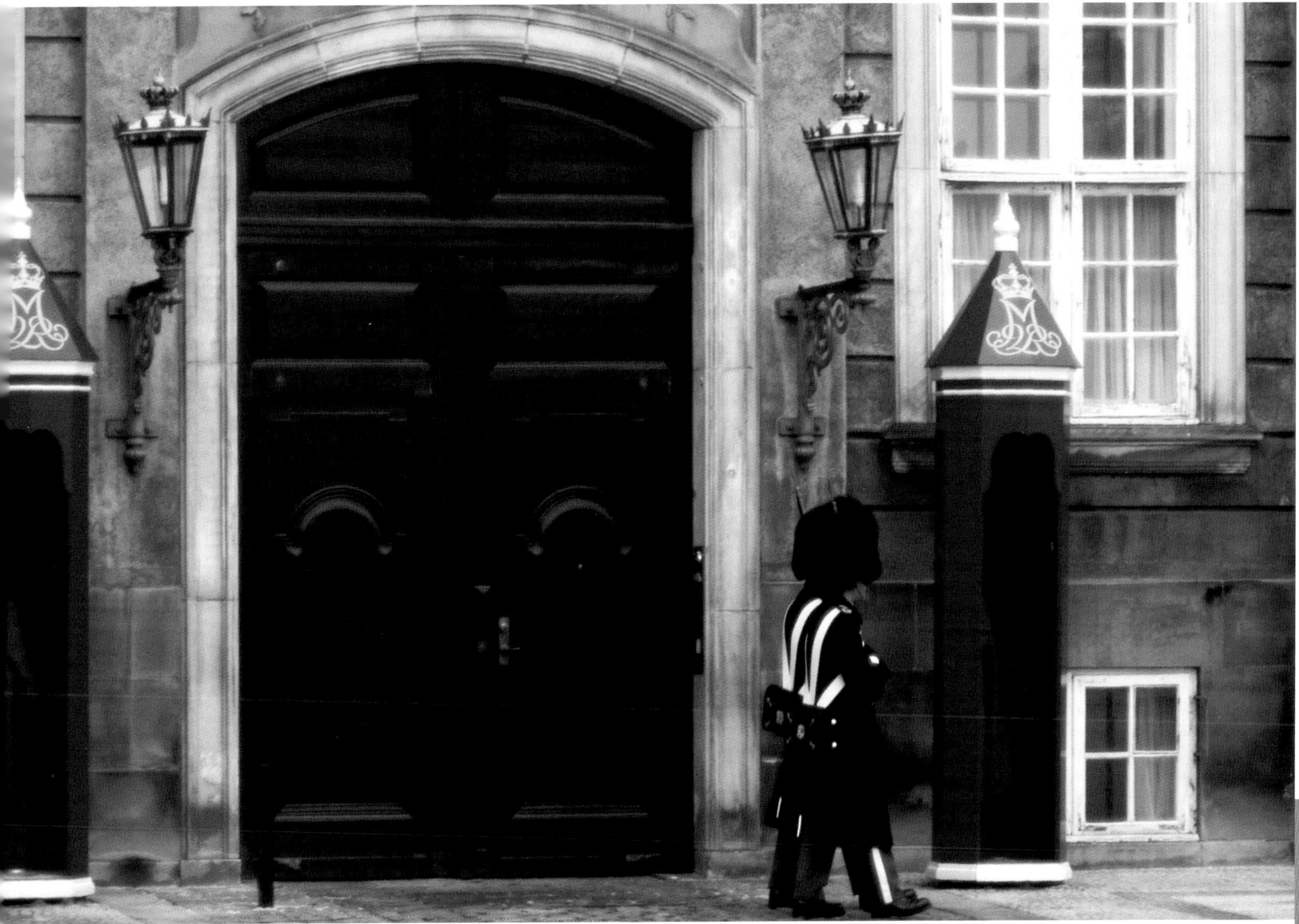

FRANCE

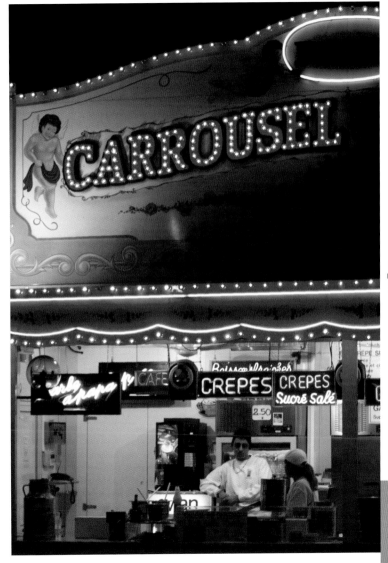

164

166

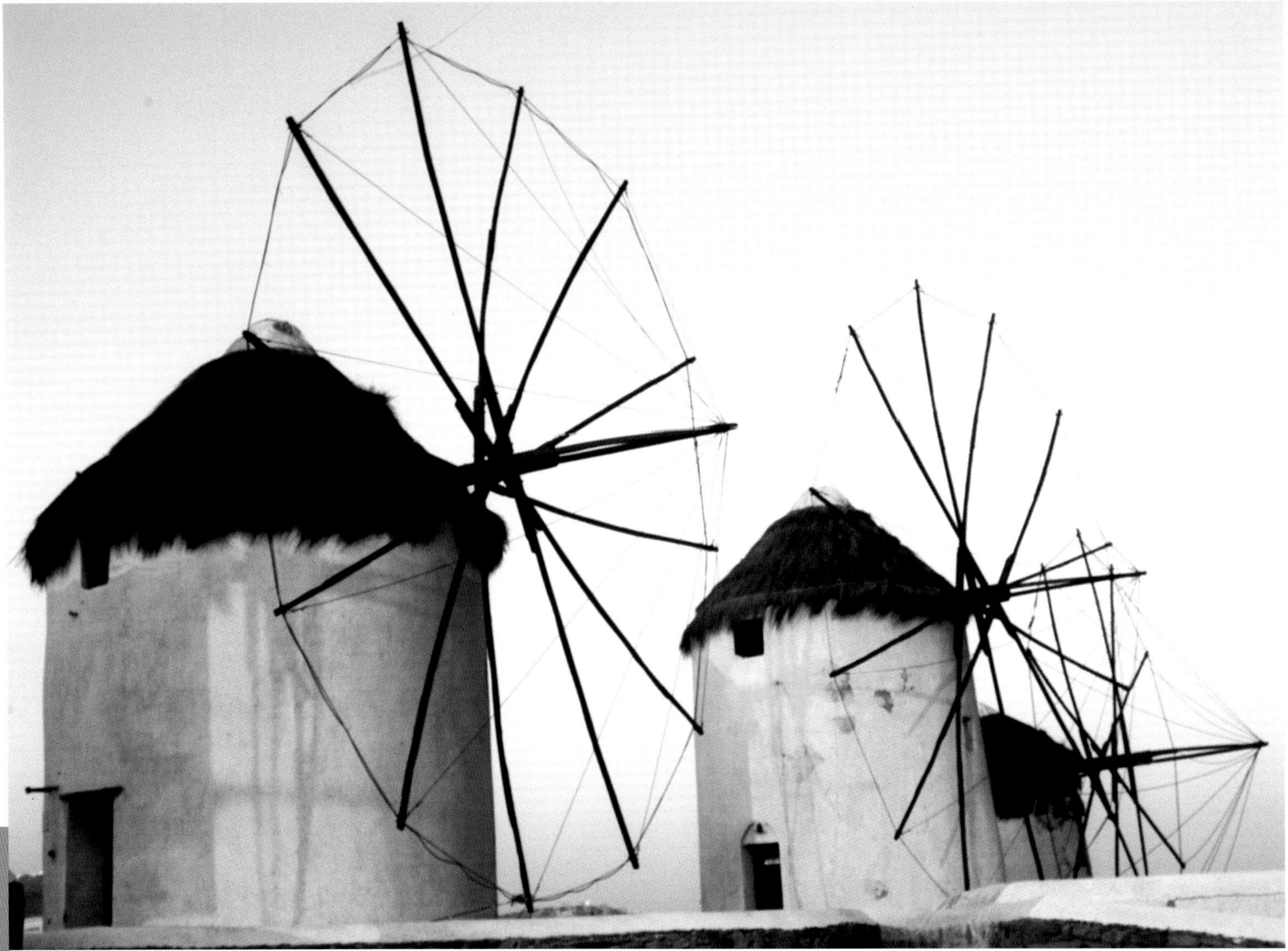

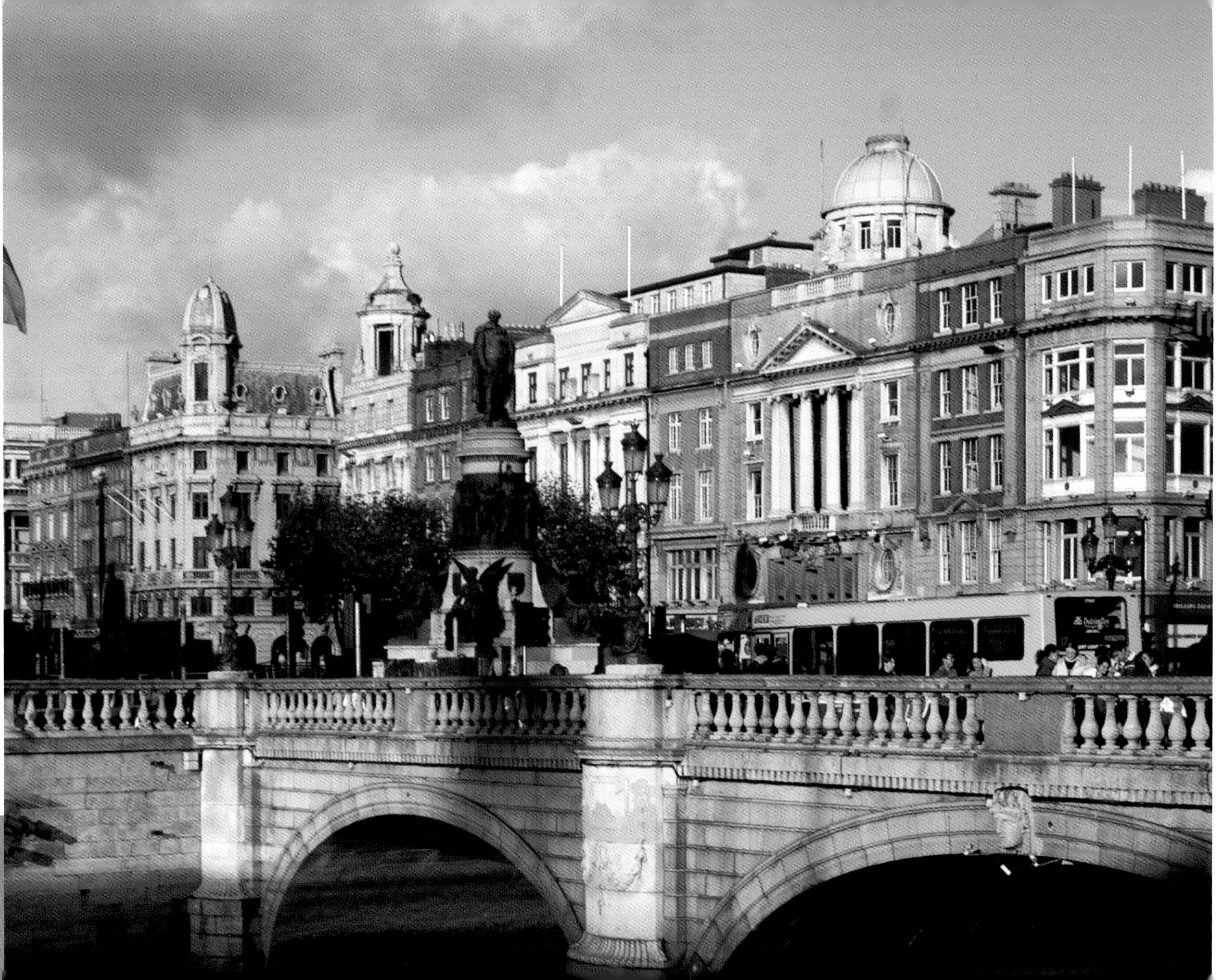

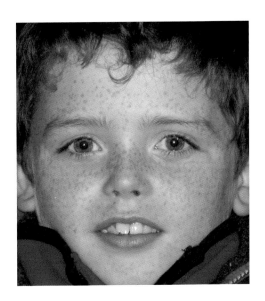

IRELAND

ITALY

187

EUROPE

ROME

TURKEY

194

UNITED KINGDOM

EUROPE

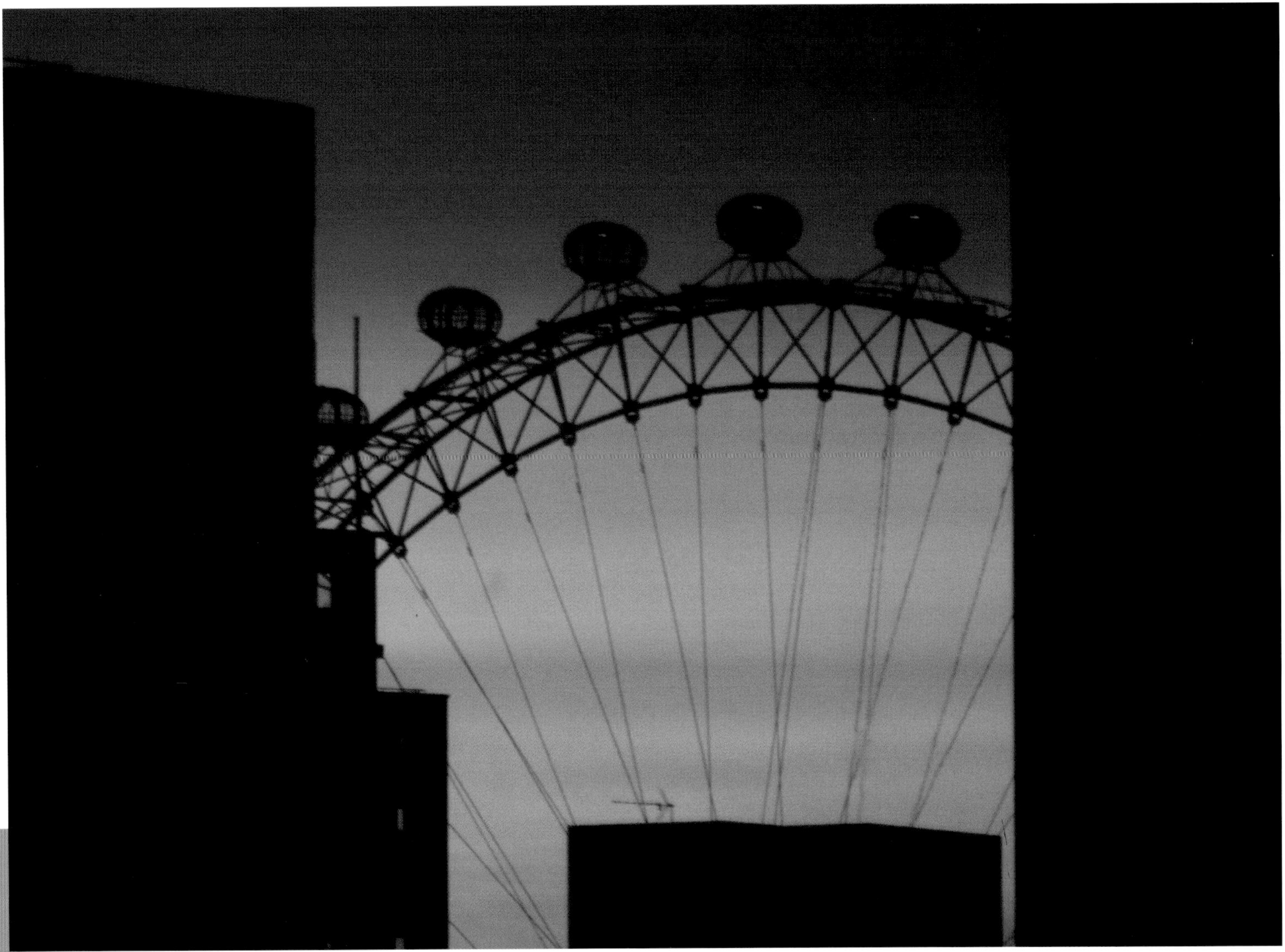

AFRICA

Algeria	Gambia	Rwanda
Angola	Ghana	Sao Tome and Principe
Benin	Guinea	Senegal
Botswana	Guinea-Bissau	Seychelles
Burkina Faso	Ivory Coast	Sierra Leone
Burundi	Kenya	Somalia
Cameroon	Lesotho	South Africa
Cape Verde	Liberia	Sudan
Central African Republic	Libya	Swaziland
Chad	Madagascar	Tanzania
Comoros	Malawi	Togo
Congo	Mali	Tunisia
Congo (Dem. Rep.)	Mauritania	Uganda
Djibouti	Mauritius	Zambia
Egypt	Morocco	Zimbabwe
Equatorial Guinea	Mozambique	
Eritrea	Namibia	
Ethiopia	Niger	
Gabon	Nigeria	

AFRICA

EGYPT

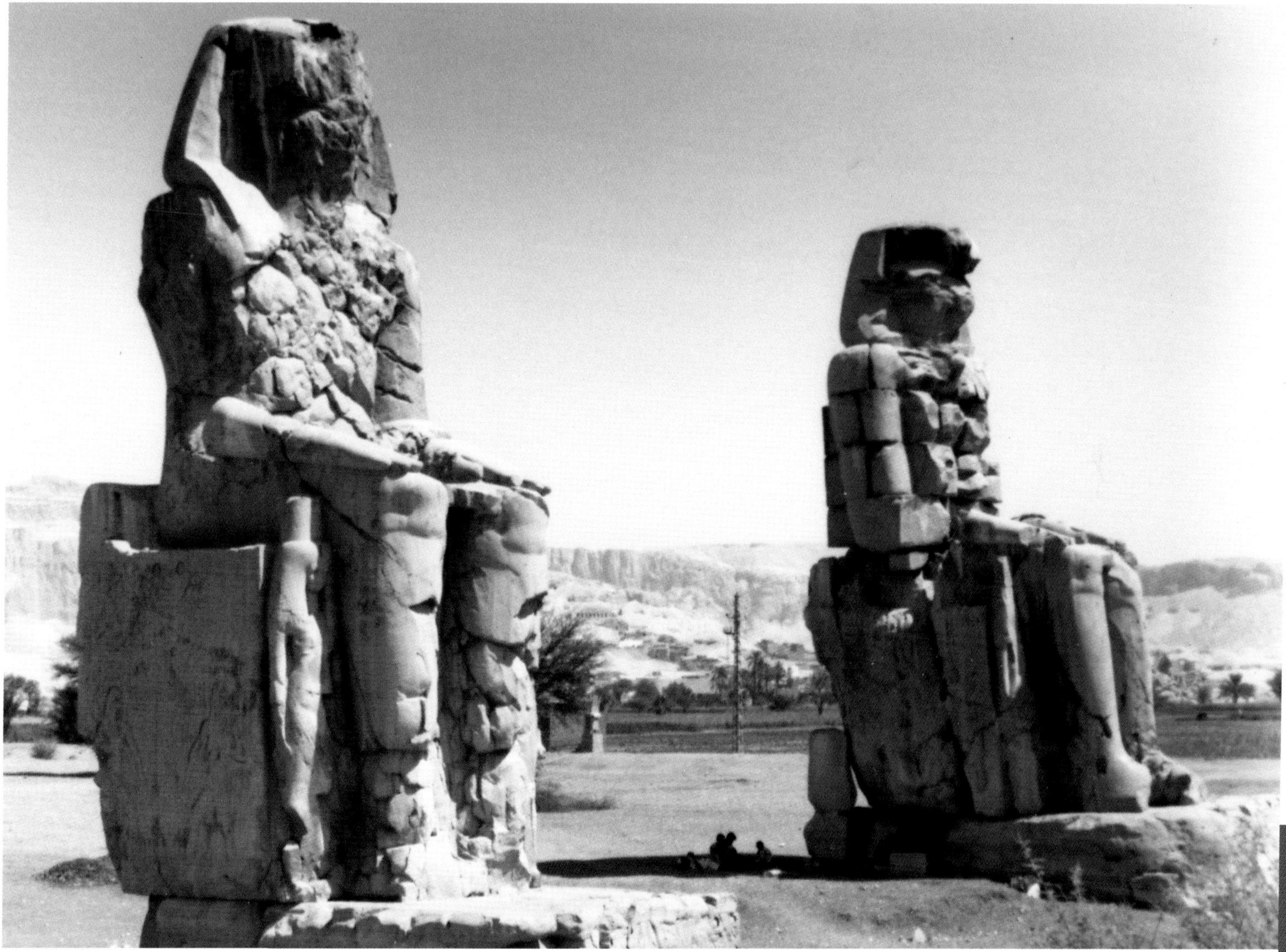

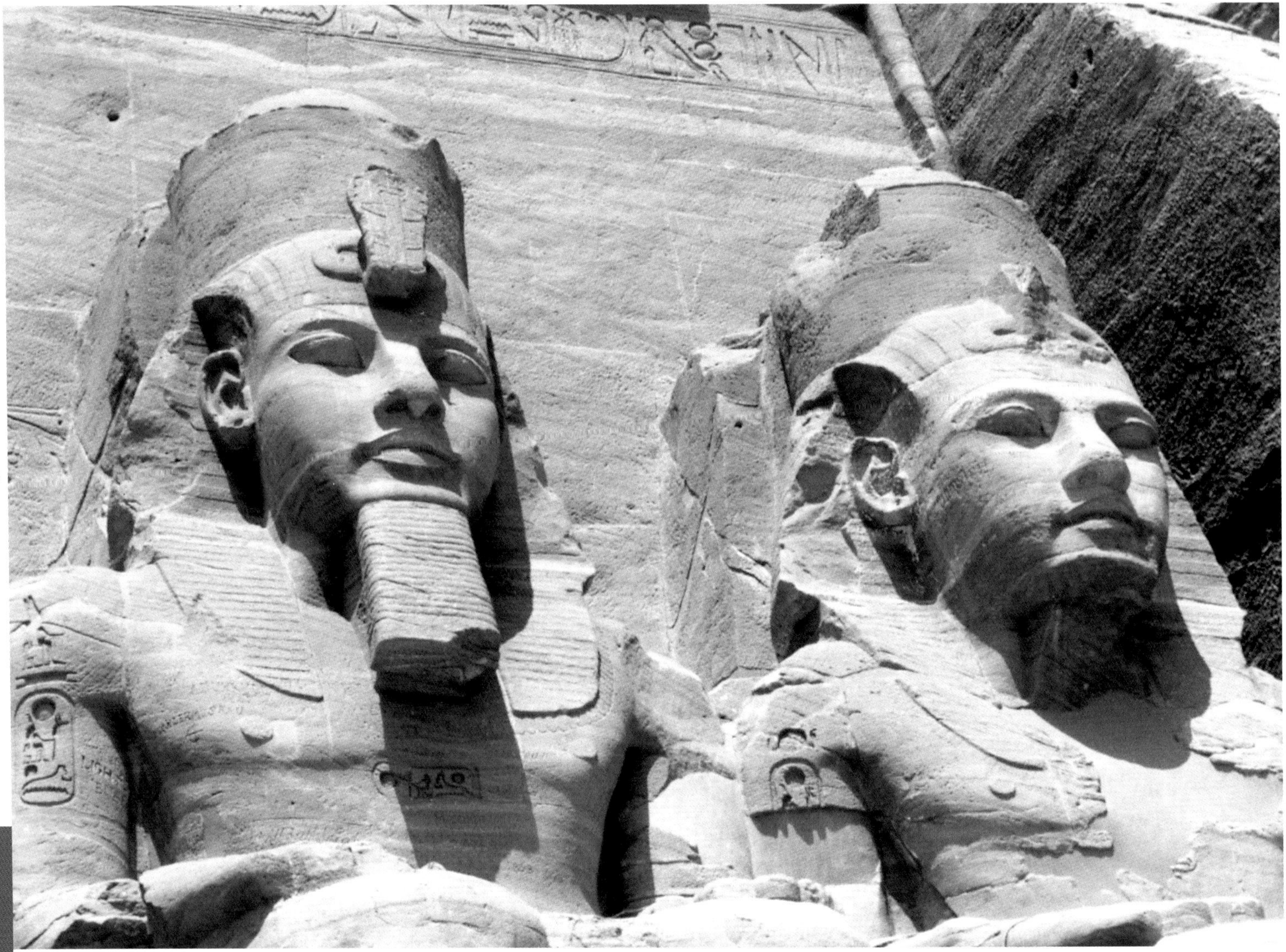

AFRICA

MOROCCO

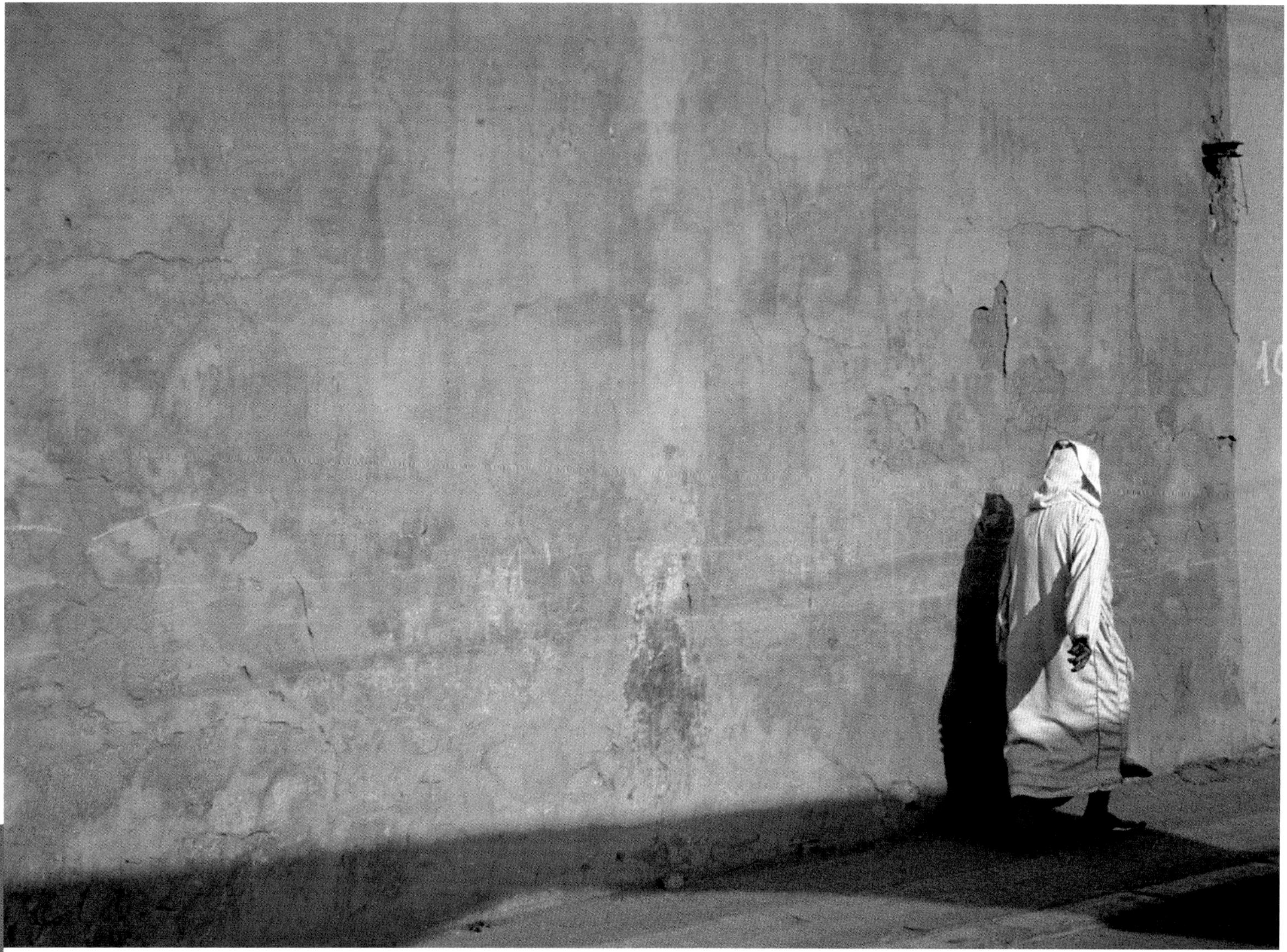

الاتحاد النسوي الوطني المغربي
لعمالات وبلدية مراكش

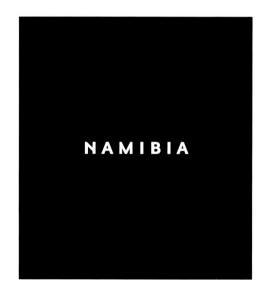

NAMIBIA

226

AFRICA

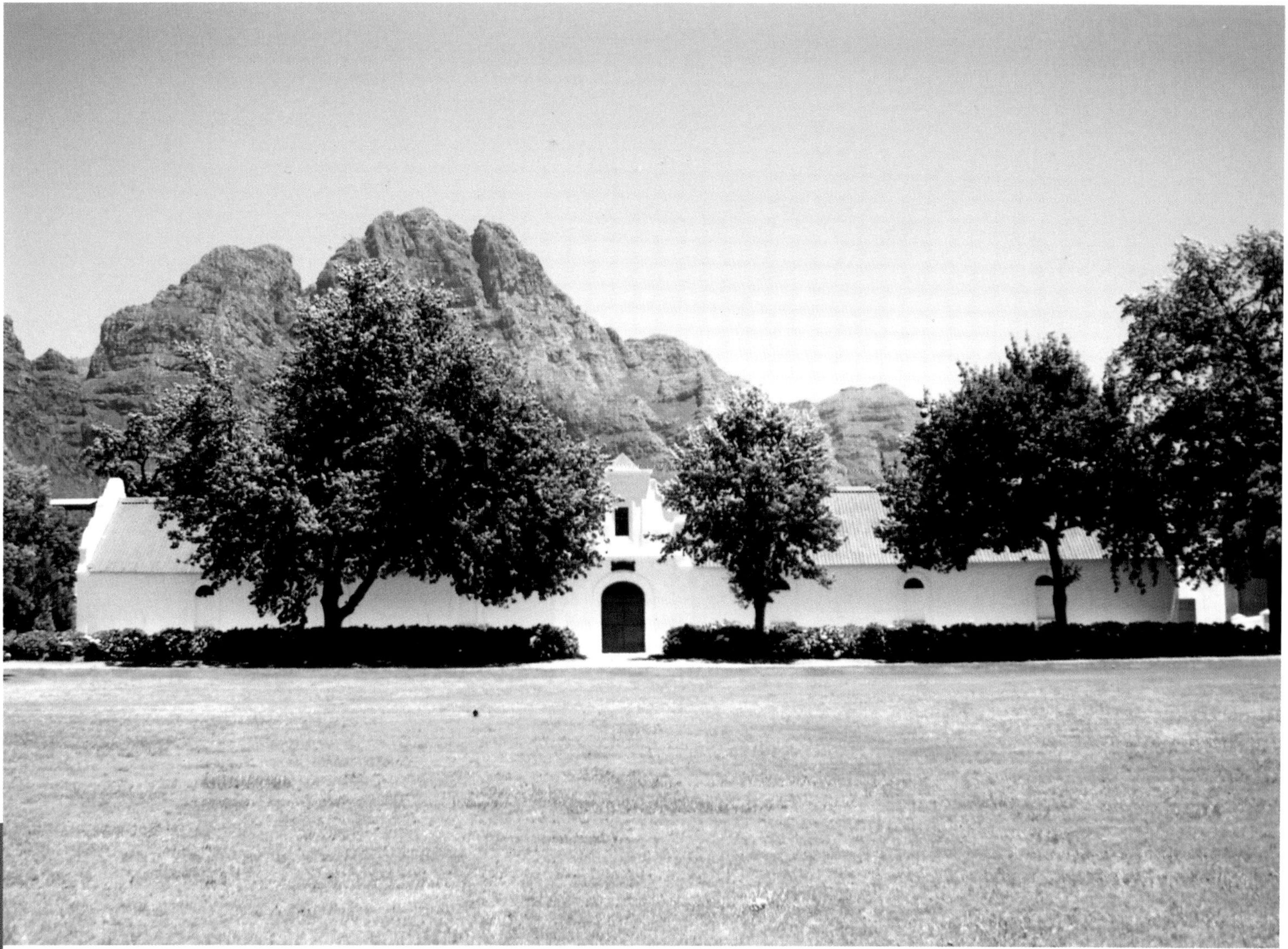

SOUTH AFRICA

TANZANIA

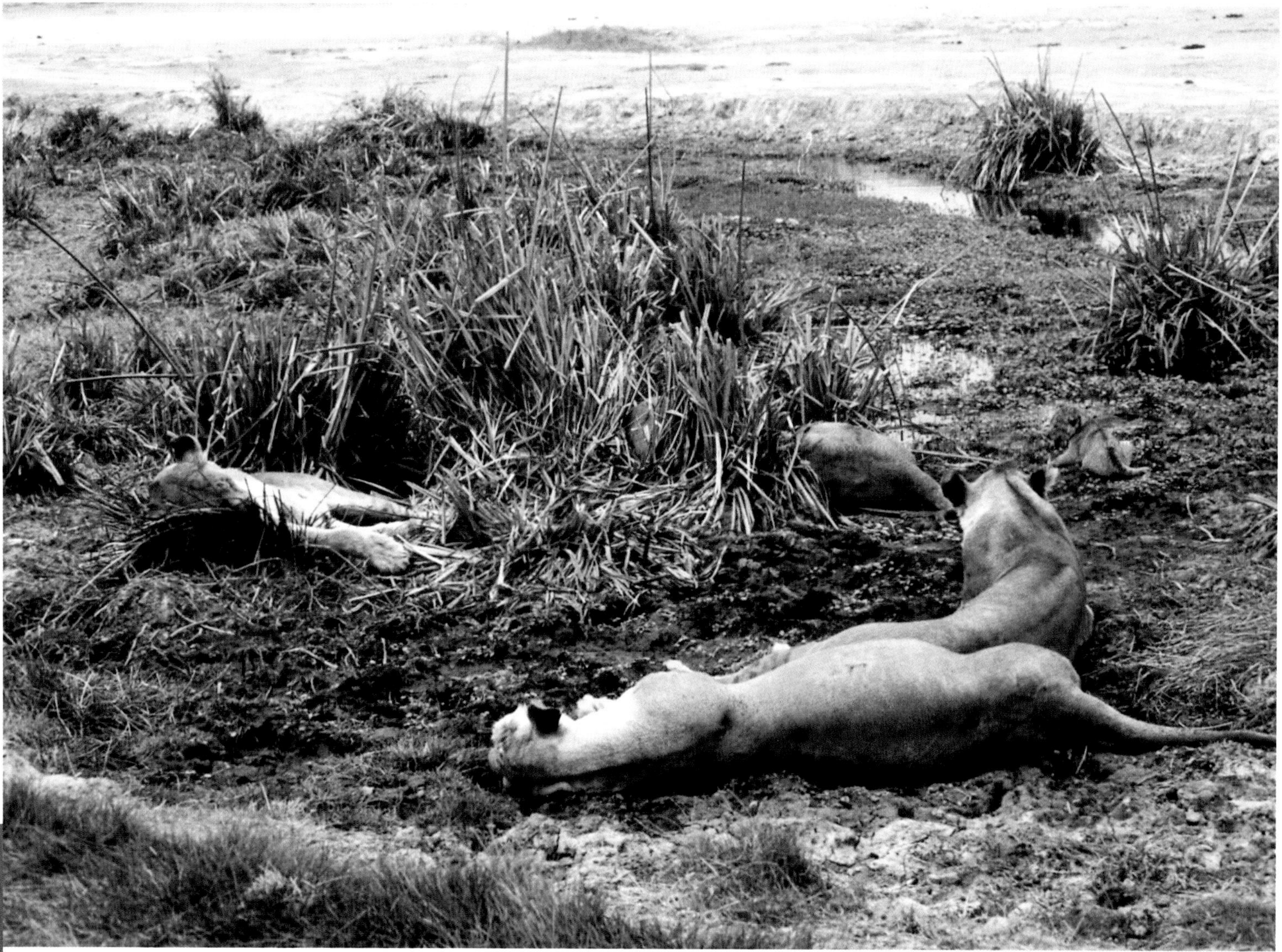

The author at Uhuru Peak. Photo by Tom DeVincentis.

OCEANIA

Australia

Fiji

Kiribati

Marshall Islands

Micronesia

Nauru

New Zealand

Palau

Papua New Guinea

Samoa

Solomon Islands

Tonga

Tuvalu

Vanuatu

OCEANIA

AUSTRALIA

OCEANIA

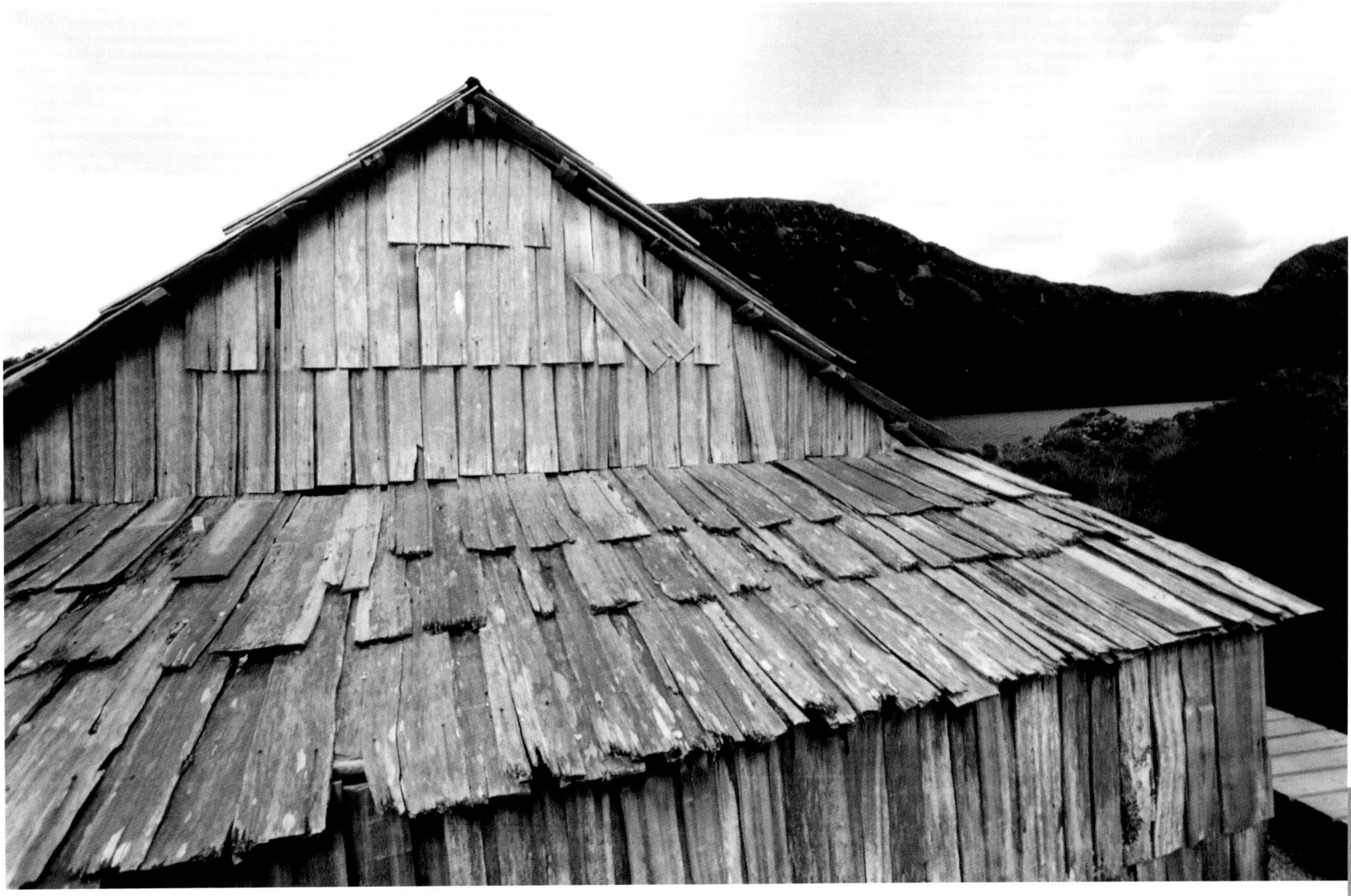

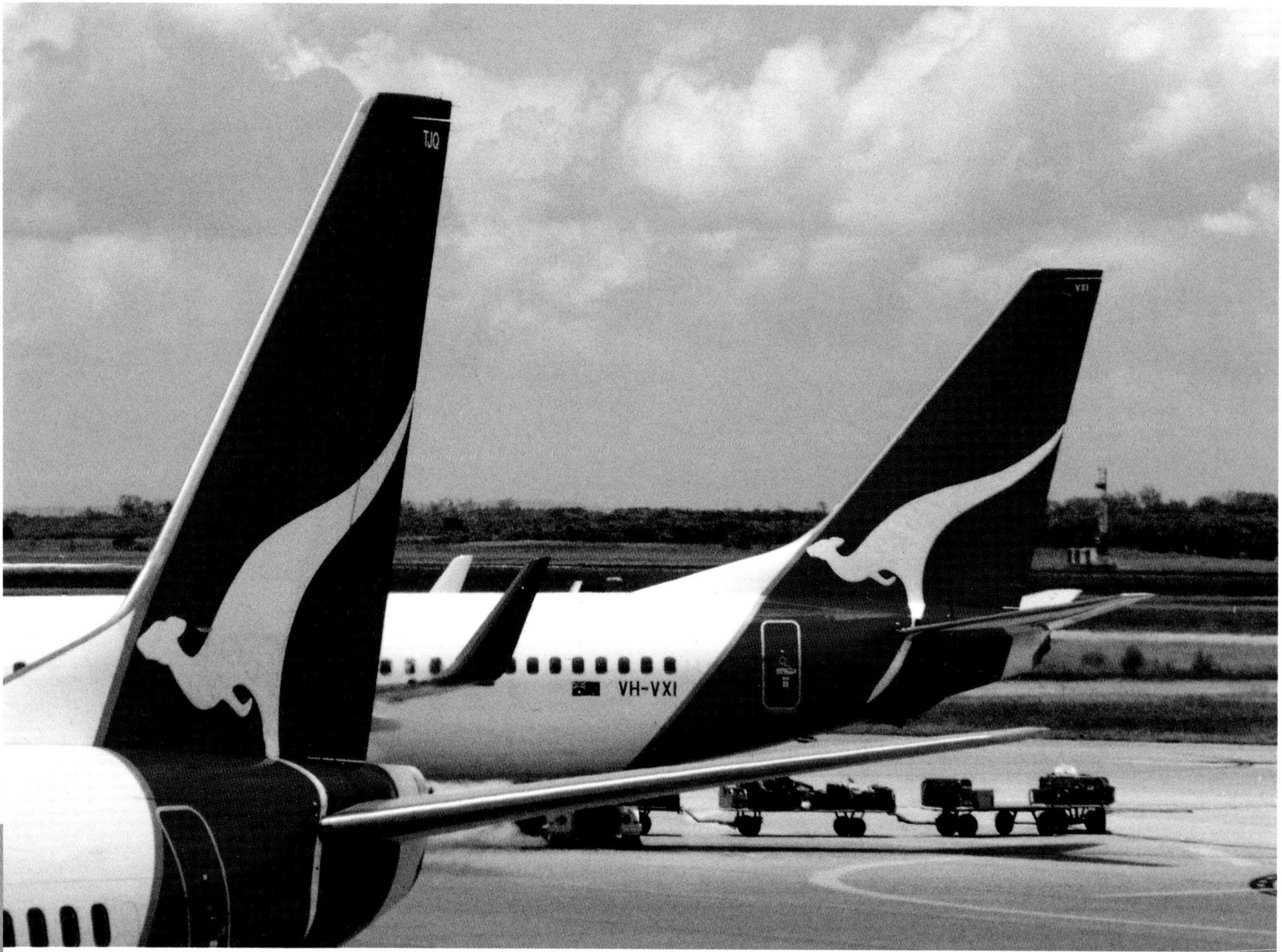
TJQ
VXI
VH-VXI

FIJI

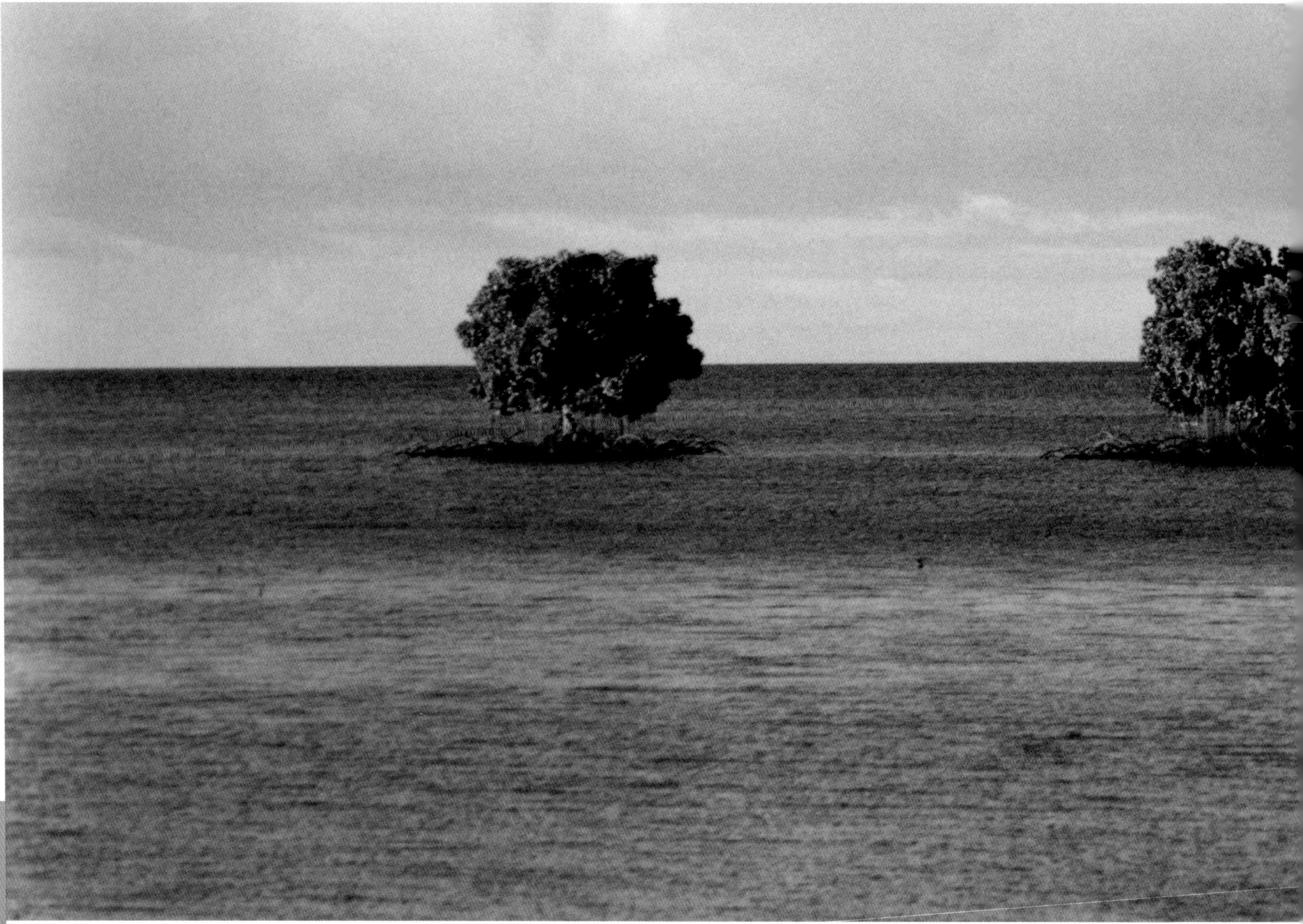

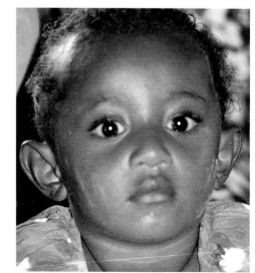

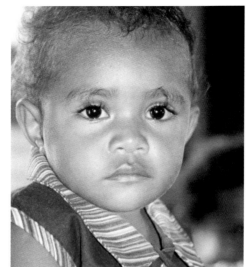

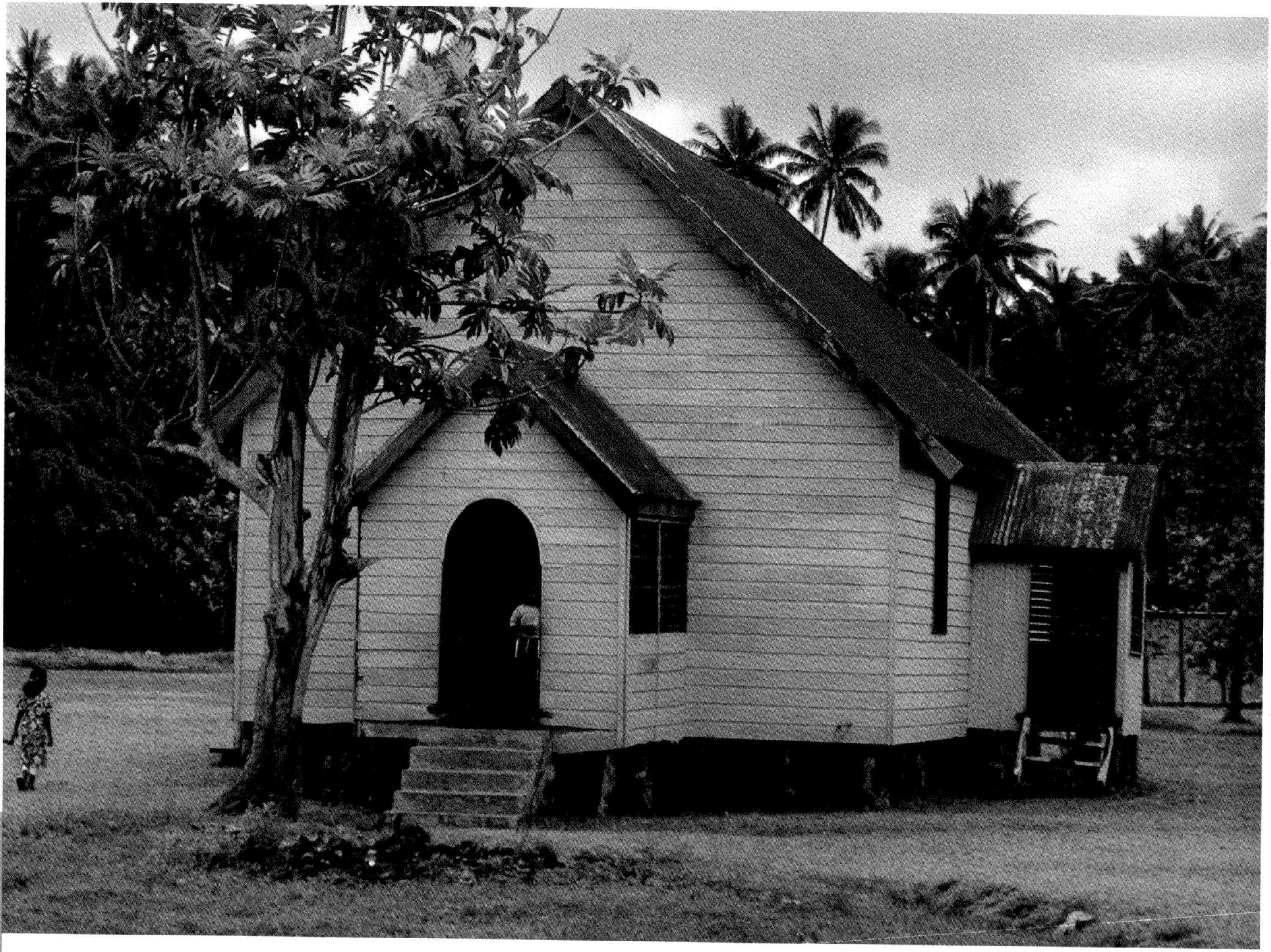

ASIA

Afghanistan	Kuwait	Thailand
Bahrain	Kyrgyzstan	Turkmenistan
Bangladesh	Laos	United Arab Emirates
Bhutan	Lebanon	Uzbekistan
Brunei	Malaysia	Vietnam
Cambodia	Maldives	Yemen
China	Mongolia	
East Timor	Myanmar (Burma)	
Hong Kong	Nepal	
India	Oman	
Indonesia	Pakistan	
Iran	Philippines	
Iraq	Qatar	
Israel	Russian Federation	
Japan	Saudi Arabia	
Jordan	Singapore	
Kazakhstan	Sri Lanka	
Korea (north)	Syria	
Korea (south)	Tajikistan	

ASIA

BHUTAN

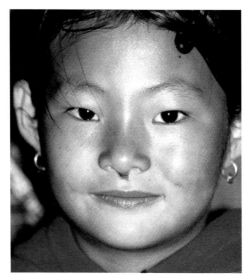

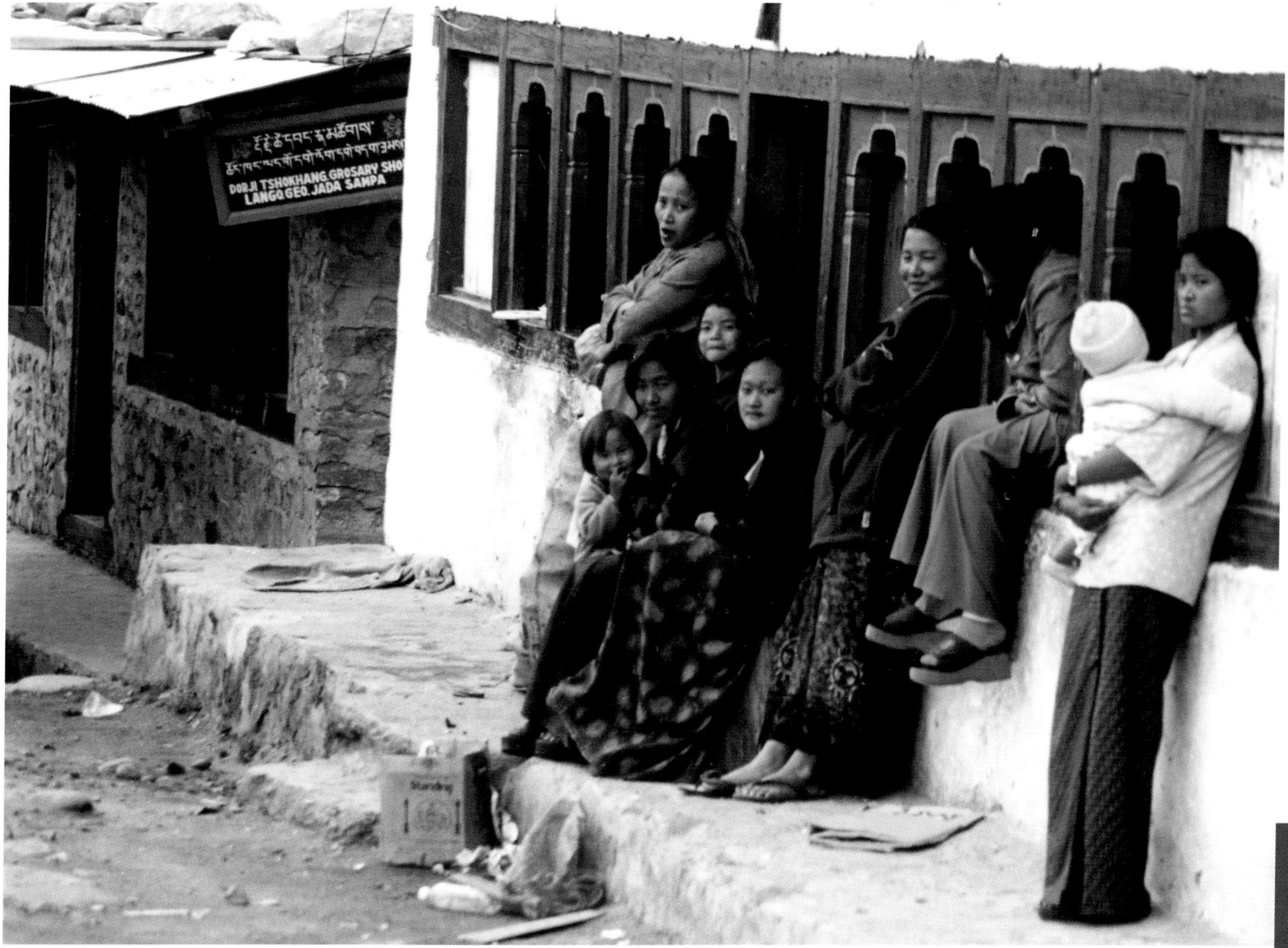
DORJI TSHOKHANG.GROSARY SHO
LANGO.GEO. JADA SAMPA

CAMBODIA

CHINA

LONGEVITY

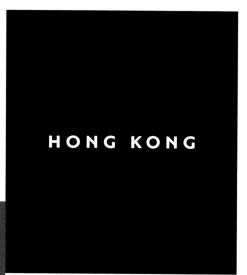

HONG KONG

歡 迎 白 色 聖 誕

INDIA

NO. 4

316

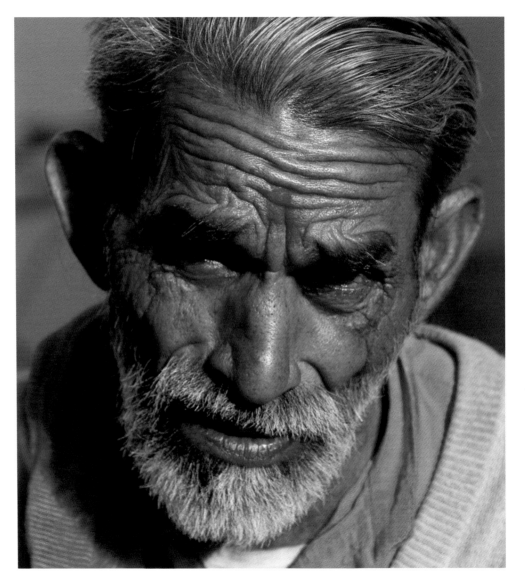

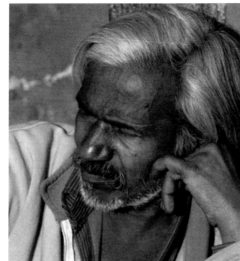

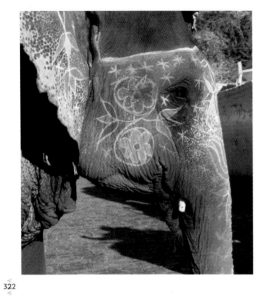

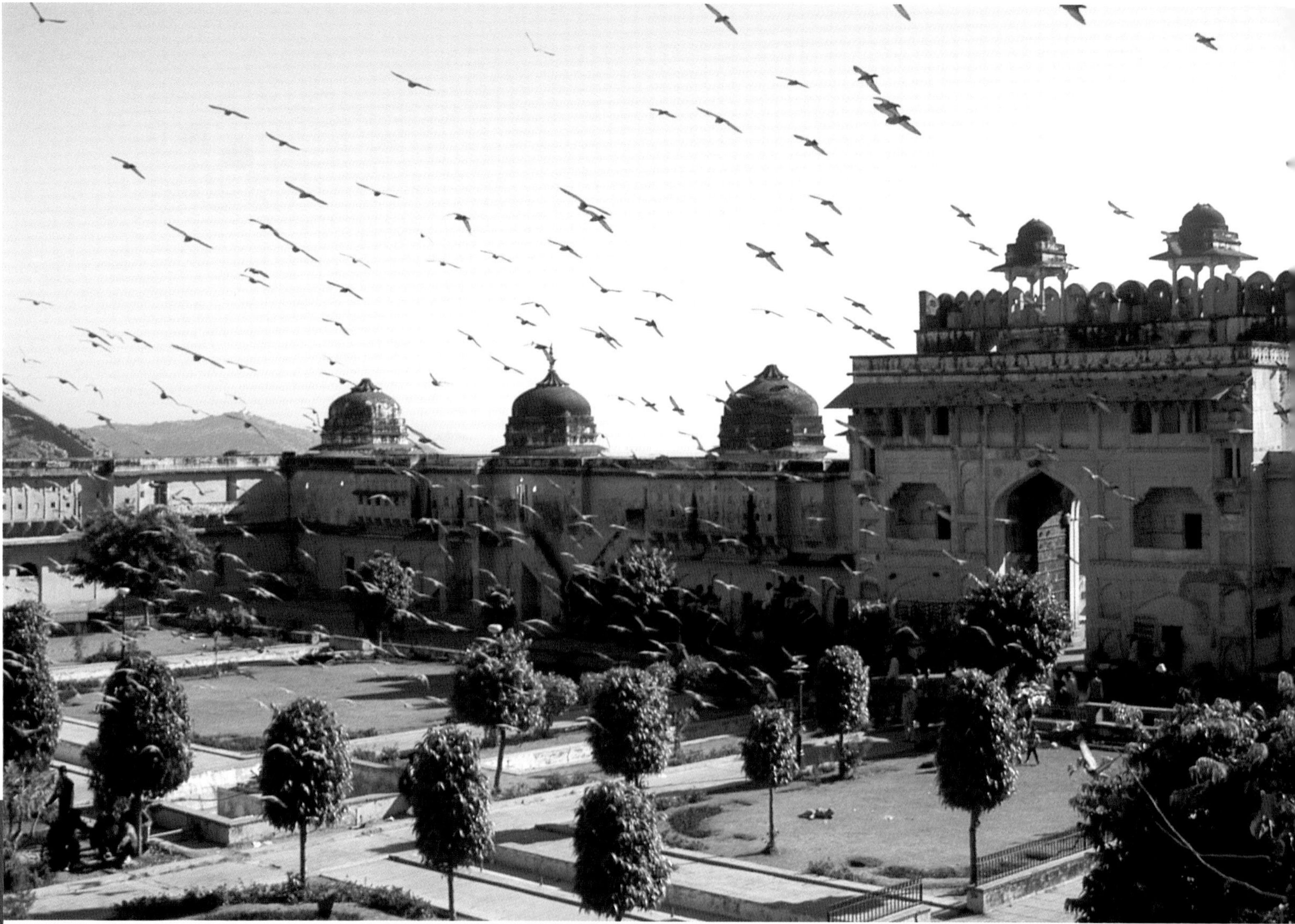

INDONESIA

JAPAN

MYANMAR
(BURMA)

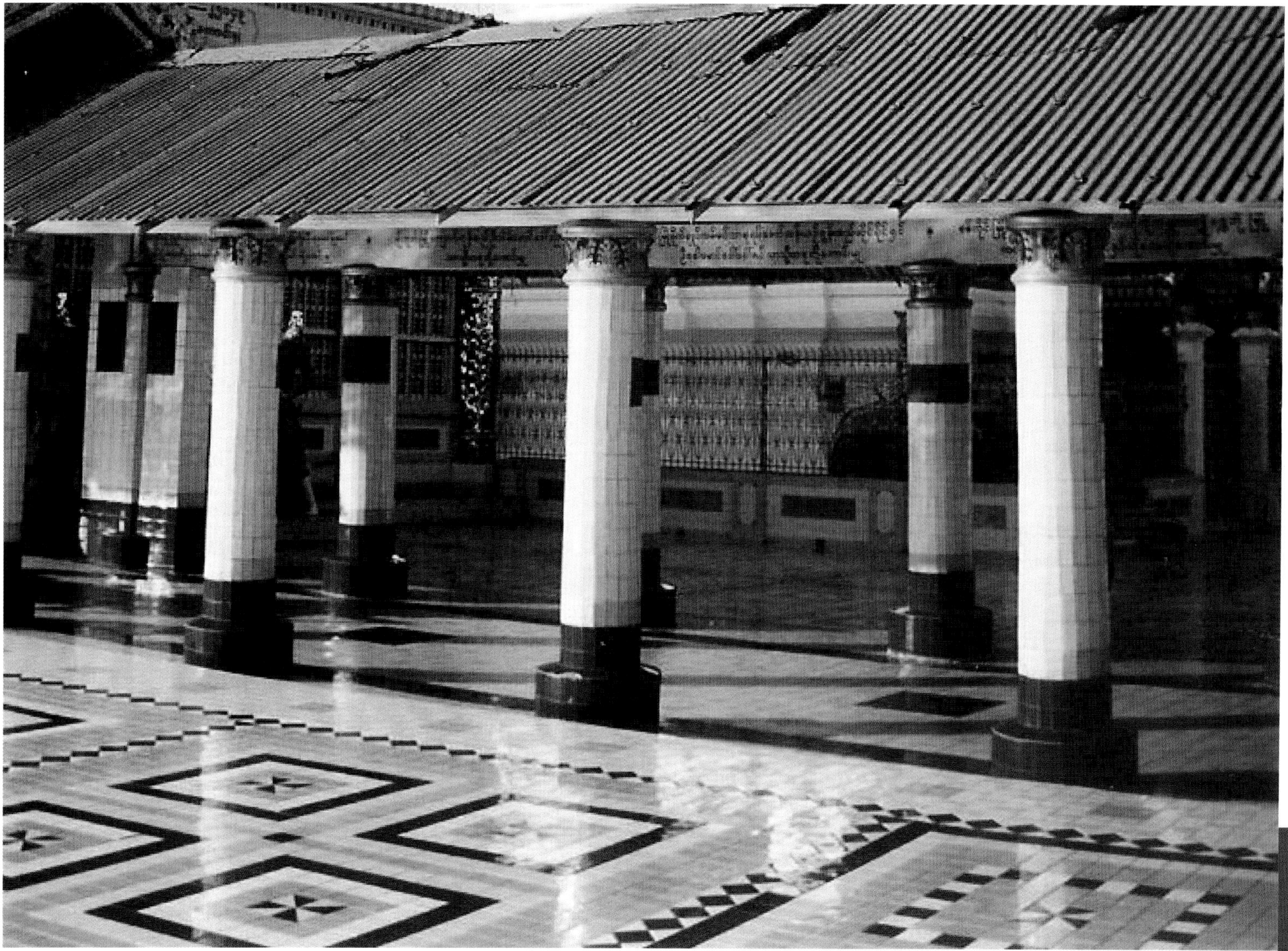

NEPAL

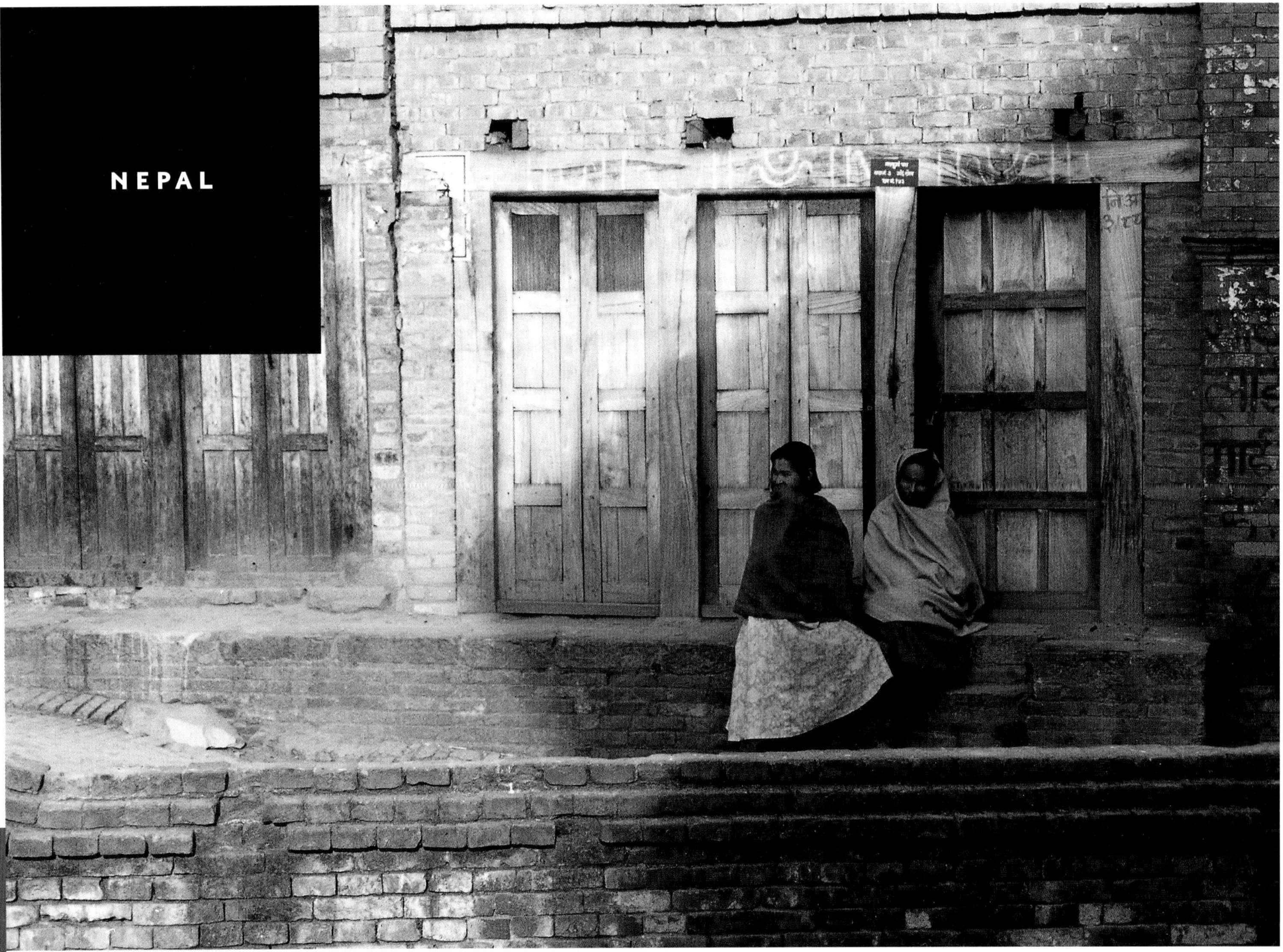

THAILAND

344

VIETNAM

ACKNOWLEDGMENTS

A special thank you to the incredible Marta Hallett for her support and guidance with this project; and to Karen Engelmann for her creative vision and to Paul Forsman for his photographer's eye.

To my fellow globetrotters who share my enthusiasm in discovering as much of the world as possible, thanks to Tom DeVincentis, Frank Valentini, Cap Sparling, Pamela Fiori, Mary Rolland, Deb Shriver, and Kate White.

To my family who have always been there to cheer me on, my gratitude to Nancy Clinton, Joseph Clinton, Kathleen Clinton, Matthew and Debbie Clinton, Chris Evans, Joe Clinton, Peg and Bob Pardini, Janet Clinton, Joanne and Michael Dimson.

And finally to those people who have encouraged and helped me along the way: thank yous to Chris Arnold, Cathie Black, Judith Bookbinder, Melissa Biggs Bradley, John Brancati, Ann Brown, Andy Carter, Francine Crane, David Granger, Amy Gross, Mac Hoak, Don Howerton, Kenro Izu, Todd Marsh, Sid and Michelle Monroe, Fred Perkins, David Schonauer, Tina Spiro, Polly Summar, Bert Tully, and Dan Tyler.

Photo of Michael Clinton by Paul Forsman.

ABOUT THE AUTHOR

MICHAEL CLINTON is Executive Vice President, Chief Marketing Officer, and Publishing Director for Hearst Magazines. His responsibilities include oversight of sixteen publications, including *Harper's Bazaar, Marie Claire, O: The Oprah Magazine, Seventeen*, and *Esquire*. Clinton serves on the board of the Starlight Foundation, having led expeditions to Nepal, Patagonia, and to the top of Mt. Kilimanjaro to raise funds for the Foundation. In addition, he is a member of the acquisitions committee of the International Center of Photography in New York City. He is also the author of WANDERLUST: ONE HUNDRED COUNTRIES (Glitterati, 2004). He lives in New York City and Southampton, New York.

PAMELA FIORI is Editor-in-Chief of *Town & Country*, the longest continuously published magazine in America, as well as Editor-in-Chief for the recently launched *Town & Country Travel* magazine. Fiori's many honors include the 1992 Melva C. Pederson Award for distinguished travel journalism and the Chevalier de l'Ordre du Mèrite, France's highest civic honor, which she received in 1985. She lives in New York City and Easthampton, New York.

Napa, California

Easthampton, NY

Here are the "favorites" lists of some well-traveled folk:

Cities: Paris, London, Rome, New York, Dublin
Man-made Places: Taj Mahal; Empire State Building; Eiffel Tower; Colosseum, Rome; Topkapi; Ice Hotel, Canada
Natural Wonders: Grand Canyon, USA; Antarctic icebergs and glaciers; Berkshire Hills, USA; Masai Mara, Kenya; Syrian escarpment
Top Travel Moments: Every time I come home and see the island of Manhattan in all its glory; floating in a hot-air balloon above the Masai Mara, Kenya; skydiving over the Berkshire Hills at peak foliage season; sailing around Cape Horn, Chile; hiking into Machu Picchu, Peru

From Melissa Biggs Bradley, Magazine Editor

Cities: Paris for its beauty; Sydney for its enthusiasm; Rome for its antiquities; New York for its energy; Cape Town for its setting
Man-made Places: Angkor Wat, Cambodia; Petra, Jordan; Great Wall, China; Taj Mahal, India; the Vatican, Rome; Sydney Opera House, Australia
Natural Wonders: Southern Alps, New Zealand, because from atop a glacier you can view a sea and a rain forest; Ha Long Bay, Vietnam, especially as you arrive from the South China Sea; the Grand Canyon, Arizona, for its enormous drama; the Serengeti Plain, Tanzania, for its wildlife; the Belize reef for idyllic and deserted tropical islands
Top Travel Moments: Skiing in Les Trois Vallées in France on a sunny day with perfect snow and ending up at a rustic farmhouse that served Michelin-starred food; exploring Angkor Wat at sunrise and seeing pilgrims arriving to worship; eating dinner on a beach on Mnemba Island, off the coast of Zanzibar, where we sat at a table set in the sand, wore no shoes, and ate marlin that my husband had caught that morning in the Indian Ocean; waking up in a private tented camp on the Serengeti in Tanzania, hundreds of miles away from any other settlement, and spending the morning in the midst of migrating animals; anytime I get to spend a few hours walking around the Left Bank of Paris, where I once lived and hope one day to live again

From Tom DeVincentis, Veterinarian

Cities: Paris, France; Venice, Italy; Oaxaca, Mexico; Aspen, Colorado; Delray Beach, Florida
Man-made Places: Pyramids of Egypt; Taj Mahal, India; Grand Canal, Venice, Italy; Pompeii, Italy; Agrigento ruins, Sicily
Natural Wonders: Canyon de Chelly, Arizona; Ngorongoro Crater, Tanzania; Galápagos Islands; dunes, Namibia; icebergs, Antarctica
Top Travel Moments: Horseback riding in Patagonia; camelback riding in Egypt; classic Turkish bath in Istanbul; the Kentucky Derby; hiking the dunes in Namibia

From Pamela Fiori, Magazine Editor-in-Chief

Favorite Destinations: Italy, France, England, India, Africa
Cities: New York; London; Paris; Venice; Rome
Man-made Places: Taj Mahal, India; the Great Sphinx and adjacent pyramids, Giza, Egypt; Machu Picchu, Peru; Piazza San Marco, Venice; Statue of Liberty, New York
Natural Wonders: Serengeti Plain, Tanzania; Grand Tetons, Colorado; northeastern United States in autumn; Yellowstone National Park, Wyoming; the turquoise waters of the Caribbean Sea
Top Travel Moments (all "firsts"): Living in Florence and traveling through Europe on my own (October 1967–February 1968), changing my life; seeing Beirut in its heyday (1972), when it was full of spies, foreign correspondents, sex appeal, and intrigue; traversing Hong Kong Harbor—the most exciting harbor on earth—on the Star Ferry between Kowloon and Hong Kong (1976); watching the sun set at the watering hole at Tsavo National Park, Kenya, a blissful moment with a thirsty gathering of baboon, warthog, zebra, Cape buffalo, and waterbuck (1982); visiting the beaches of Normandy and the American Cemetery (1983)—the memory of seeing all those thousands of gravesites still makes me weep.

From Paul Forsman, Photographer

Cities: Paris; Rome; Paia, Hawaii; New York; Bangkok, Thailand
Man-made Places: New York Public Library; Palace of

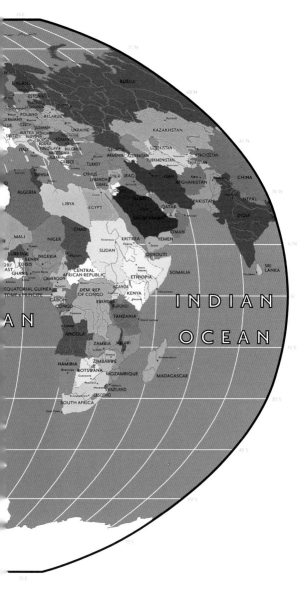

INDIAN

OCEAN

FAVORITE PLACES: MINE AND OTHERS

What is it that makes a city someone's "favorite," or what man-made structure or natural wonder has stopped you in your tracks? What travel experience has touched you in a way that you savor it, or think about it, as one of your life's best moments ever? If you are well-traveled, it's hard to isolate a handful, especially for me, because my list is long. Here are my answers:

CITIES

Bangkok, Thailand
Bologna, Italy
Cape Town, South Africa
Istanbul, Turkey
Jaipur, India
Jerusalem, Israel
Kathmandu, Nepal
Marrakech, Morocco
Miami, FL, USA
New York, NY, USA
Paris, France
Rome, Italy
Santa Fe, NM, USA
Sydney, Australia
Vancouver, Canada

MANMADE PLACES

Amber Fort, India
Angkor Wat, Cambodia
Borobudur, Indonesia
Chrysler Building, USA
Eiffel Tower, France
Grand Palace, Thailand
Hagia Sophia, Turkey
Karnak Temple, Egypt
Library of Celsius, Turkey
Machu Picchu, Peru
Pagan, Myanmar
Piazza Navona, Italy
Shwedagon Pagoda, Myanmar
Taj Mahal, India

NATURAL WONDERS

Antarctic Peninsula, Antarctica
Arches National Park, Utah, USA
Canyon de Chelly, Arizona, USA
Cape of Good Hope, South Africa
Dunes, Namibia
Grand Canyon, Arizona, USA
Mt. Kilimanjaro, Tanzania
Ngorongoro Crater, Tanzania
Perito Moreno Glacier, Argentina
Serengeti Plain, Tanzania
Skeleton Coast, Namibia
Sugarloaf Mountain, Brazil
Taos Pueblo, New Mexico, USA
Victoria Falls, Zambia

Yellowstone National Park, Wyoming, USA

TOP TRAVEL MOMENTS

• Arriving at Angkor Wat at dawn
• Arriving at the top of Mt. Kosciusko, the tallest mountain in Australia
• Awakening to a rainbow on Christmas morning on the island of Nukubati in Fiji
• Biking on the red rocks in Arches National Park, Utah, USA
• Flying over the Namibian sand dunes and the Skeleton Coast in a single-engine plane
• Ice climbing on the Perito Moreno Glacier in Patagonia, Argentina
• Seeing the Eiffel Tower for the first time as a teenager
• Sleeping in the open air on the Antarctic Peninsula
• Standing at the top of Mt. Kilimanjaro as the sun rises over Africa
• Swimming with the dolphins in the Galápagos Islands
• Trekking in the Annapurnas in Nepal

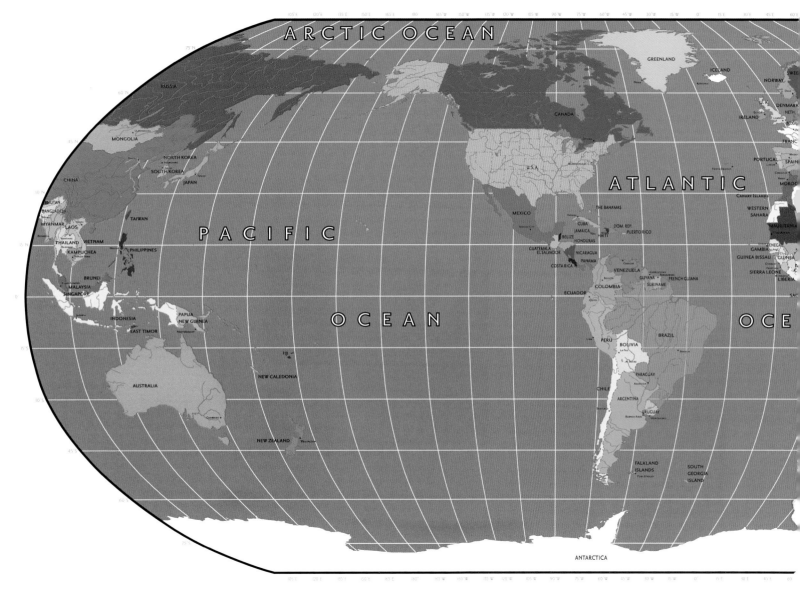

Versailles, France; Monument to Vittorio Emanuele II, Rome; Our Lady of Angels Cathedral, Los Angeles; Millennium Bridge, London

NATURAL WONDERS: Grand Canyon, Arizona; Mt. Aconcagua, Argentina; Molokai coastline, Hawaii; the Irish countryside; Big Sur, California

TOP TRAVEL MOMENTS: Exploring the Tuscan countryside; windsurfing on the Columbia River; traveling through northern Vermont in the fall; surfing in Maui; sunset in the Italian hilltop town of Cortona

FROM KENRO IZU, PHOTOGRAPHER

FAVORITE DESTINATION: Kingdom of Bhutan

CITIES: Varanasi, India; Luang Prabang, Laos; Cairo, Egypt; Patan, Nepal

MAN-MADE PLACES: Pyramids at Giza, Egypt; Angkor Wat, Cambodia; Machu Picchu, Peru; Silk Road, China; Elora, Canada

NATURAL WONDERS: Mt. Kailash, Tibet; Urubamba River and surrounding mountains, Peru; Petra Valley, Jordan; mustangs in Nepal; River Ganges, India

TOP TRAVEL MOMENTS: The first morning sun on Mt. Kailash, Tibet; the view from a mountaintop on a mustang trek; watching sunset with an old guide at Patan; meeting with children at Angkor Wat; being stuck in a tent at Kailash circuit for five days due to snow and fog

FROM JACK KLIGER, PUBLISHING EXECUTIVE

CITIES: Paris, Florence, Venice, New York, San Francisco

MAN-MADE PLACES: Piazza San Marco, Venice; Il Duomo, Florence; Tulum, Mexico; Red Square, Moscow

NATURAL WONDERS: Watch Hill beach, Rhode Island; Hanalei Bay, Kauai, Hawaii; Sugarloaf Mountain, Rio de Janeiro; Old Faithful geyser, Yellowstone National Park, Wyoming

TOP TRAVEL MOMENTS: Drinking all night at a bar in the zocalo in Oaxaca, Mexico; strolling along Ipanema Beach

in Rio de Janeiro and meeting the (real) girl from Ipanema; walking through the gardens at Giverny, France; sitting in a field in the Cotswolds, England, eating wild blackberries; listening to Gregorian chants at the church of San Miniato al Monte in Florence

FROM CHRIS RAINIER, PHOTOGRAPHER

CITIES: Rio de Janeiro, Brazil; San Francisco, California; Sydney, Australia; Varanasi, India; Bhaktapur, Nepal

MAN-MADE PLACES: Statues on Easter Island, Chile; Machu Picchu, Peru; Petra, Jordan; Angkor Wat, Cambodia; Meroë pyramids, Sudan

NATURAL WONDERS: Antarctica; deserts of the Sahara; Polynesian sunrise; full moon at the Taj Mahal, India; sunset at Santa Fe, New Mexico

The author in Bhutan. Photo by Frank Valentini.

FROM DEB SHRIVER, CORPORATE COMMUNICATIONS OFFICER

CITIES: New York; Paris; New Orleans; Venice; London

MAN-MADE PLACES: Lincoln Memorial, Washington, D.C.; Palace of Fine Arts, San Francisco; Literary Walk in Central Park, New York; Chartres Street, New Orleans; all the monuments in Rome

NATURAL WONDERS: Kalahari Desert Basin, Botswana; Gulf of Mexico along Perdido Key, Florida; swamps surrounding Lafayette, Louisiana; Mississippi Delta; sands of Kitty Hawk, North Carolina

TOP TRAVEL MOMENTS: Watching a mother cheetah feed and then bathe her cub in the confines of Kruger National Park, South Africa; watching a pride of three sister lionesses troop their five cubs through a wildlife sanctuary in South Africa while being stalked by their brother, a hungry lion; witnessing the adoption of tsunami-orphaned children by their immediate family members, gathered together in a makeshift tent in Phuket, Thailand; sleeping and dining by candlelight in the Kalahari Desert in Namibia— "sans" tent, but with a bed, linens, candelabra, and open fire; the first visit to Venice, Italy

FROM FRANK VALENTINI, TELEVISION PRODUCER

CITIES: Cape Town, South Africa; Florence, Italy; Sydney, Australia; Marrakech, Morocco; Bangkok, Thailand

MAN-MADE PLACES: Taj Mahal, India; Angkor Wat, Cambodia; Chrysler Building, New York City; Musée d'Orsay, Paris; Karnak Temple, Egypt

NATURAL WONDERS: Victoria Falls, South Africa; Grand Canyon, Arizona

TOP TRAVEL MOMENTS: Walking into Sossusvlei, Namibia; landing in a seaplane near Nukubati Island, Fiji; visiting Luxor, Egypt; flying to Paris for a weekend with my best friend; traveling up the Mekong Delta in Vietnam on my way to Siem Reap to eventually see Angkor Wat

I hope that my lists of favorite places and my photographic record of them, along with the lists of some of these seasoned travelers, will inspire others to start, continue, or conclude their own lists and create their own GLOBAL SNAPS. — MICHAEL A. CLINTON